DATE			

SECURITY DURING STRIKES

SECURITY
DURING STRIKES

By

James W. Wensyel

CHARLES C THOMAS • PUBLISHER
Springfield • Illinois • U.S.A.

Published and Distributed Throughout the World by

CHARLES C THOMAS • PUBLISHER
2600 South First Street
Springfield, Illinois 62717

With THOMAS BOOKS *careful attention is given to all details of manufacturing and
design. It is the Publisher's desire to present books that are satisfactory as to their physical
qualities and artistic possibilities and appropriate for their particular use.* THOMAS
BOOKS *will be true to those laws of quality that assure a good name and good will.*

Library of Congress Cataloging in Publication Data

Wensyel, James W.
 Security during strikes.

 Bibliography: p.
 Includes index.
 1. Strikes and lockouts. 2. Industry—Security
measures. I. Title.
HD5306.W46 1985 658.4'73 85–8032
ISBN 0-398-05149-6

Printed in the United States of America
SC-R-3

James W. Wensyel directed law enforcement, investigative and industrial security programs for the U.S. Army for more than twenty years. He subsequently served as Director of Security for several international corporations and continues to work as a security consultant.

For three whose caring made so much possible: Catherine E. Shirk, godmother; Vera E. Wensyel, mother; Jean S. Wensyel, wife.

PREFACE

Many managers are reluctant to admit the existence of security problems—theft, fraud, embezzlement, misuse of company property—in their companies. Most, however, will readily admit concern for the damage a strike, whether of violent or non-violent character, can cause.

Most companies have no professionally trained Security Director. That function is an additional duty assigned to the Personnel Director, the Director of Industrial Relations, or to another manager. In many cases these individuals are not trained in general security matters, let alone in the specifics of security during a strike. Even professional Security Directors may not be experienced in these specifics.

Because responsible individuals are not fully aware of security aspects of strike management they do not realize defensive measures they might take before or during a strike to minimize its impact. The absence of planning and preparation thus leads to on-the-spot decisions and make-do operations that can aggravate inevitable confrontations and cause others.

This book develops concepts of security during strikes and provides sufficient operational details to make possible the establishment of effective security measures that will minimize strike damage. The information provided also may bring to administrators not normally associated with security matters a better understanding of a company's overall protection needs and the measures by which they can be established.

This book then may be of help to management generalists, to security specialists, and to internes in the administrative or security fields.

The author acknowledges with thanks the assistance of the Indiana State Chamber of Commerce in granting permission to quote from its excellent pamphlets "Employer's Labor Relations Guidebook" and "Management During Strikes," as cited in the text.

INTRODUCTION

Most individuals responsible for directing corporate security and public safety programs have limited experience administering those programs during strikes. During the usual "quiet times" they often find themselves so busy with other projects (and security may be a "second hat" to those other responsibilities) that it's easy to rationalize that they just don't have time to prepare strike management plans or to rehearse their security staffs in those plans. Besides, it may never happen to their company anyway. If a strike does occur, however, they may find themselves with little time to prepare for it and limited knowledge of what to expect from it or how to handle problems it will present.

Even if they have had time to survey the usual security posture of their company, a strike situation is an entirely new ball game for them and for their staff. Routine Standing Operating Procedures no longer apply. Key individuals throughout the management staff will be absent or otherwise unable to perform their usual duties. Staff organizations will change. Emergency staffs and non-striking workers will work under pressures new to them, pressures that often will be very personal as old friends find themselves on opposite sides of a picket line.

The Security Director (or whoever is responsible for the corporate security and public safety programs) has a far better chance of meeting his peacekeeping responsibilities in this type situation if he has experienced a strike or been personally briefed on what to expect during one and how some problems might be avoided or, if encountered, best handled.

This text supplies that orientation. It cannot cover every situation that might arise because every strike creates its own happenings, but it focuses upon those areas and operations most affected by a strike and suggests means by which corporate security and public safety can be most easily maintained.

The Security Director or general manager should read it carefully and thoughtfully, applying its suggestions to his own corporate environment. He then should develop security aspects of a strike management plan for his company. He should put those concepts in writing and orient his security staff on them. If he has done that and a strike is imminent, he and his staff will be ready for its challenge. And he can better assist overall management planning for the strike. If a strike comes without warning, he will at least know the directions he should move to do his part in maintaining or restoring order, in preventing or containing damage, in helping restore good feeling when the conflict is resolved.

CONTENTS

SECURITY DURING STRIKES

CHAPTER 1

THE AMERICAN LABOR MOVEMENT

For more than 200 years, Americans have been quick to defend their political freedoms. In two separate instances, for eight years between 1775–1783 and for four years between 1861–1865, they fought long and terrible national wars to determine the nature and direction of their political structure. Often friend was pitted against friend, brother against brother. Not surprisingly, during these same 200 years working men and women have been equally willing to contest their economic bosses. These economic bosses, as ruggedly individualistic as the workers, in turn defended what they considered to be their rights and the rights of the companies they governed.

The national wars brought death, destruction and great suffering to many thousands of people. But they determined the nature of our government, and our people remained politically free.

The conflict between manager and worker also has been long and violent—periods of uneasy calm shattered by sometimes prolonged fire fights of various weapons and tactics. It too brought a good-sized share of suffering. But it also won something: greater rewards to the individual worker—rewards he otherwise might not have had.

Labor itself has become a big and powerful business, capable of influencing the government and the nation's commerce to considerable degree. More than fifty unions maintain large national offices in Washington. Almost under the shadow of the Capitol, the American Federation of Labor-Congress of Industrial Organizations (AF of L–CIO) union devoted $4,000,000 to its national headquarters. Nearby, the International Brotherhood of Teamsters' building topped this by a $1,000,000. And the Baker's and Confectionary Workers Union put $6,000,000 of their union funds into their Washington office. From these centers, unions direct intense lobbying efforts against the Congress and various state legislatures. They greatly influence our national electoral processes. They invest millions of union dollars in building projects, health centers, banks, summer resorts. They are big; they are wealthy; they are powerful.

Periodically we read of union funds allegedly diverted into illegal or suspect activities or into the pockets of union representatives. Or a particular union or combination of unions will take an action that devastates an industry or area until the dispute is resolved or sputters out. Then leaders of industry, commerce, government—and many private citizens—will say that labor has gone too far, demanded too much, been given too much.

Or we will hear of thousands of workers laid off or fired by the closing of a local plant, with hoped for retirement benefits earned over many years' hard work wiped out by the snap of the padlock on the plant's gate. And we will wonder at the seeming callousness of "big business." Obviously, there are two sides to the coin.

The violence sparked by both sides over the years, and the use of unethical or illegal tactics to gain perceived ends, have lessened of late as federal and state legislation established formal ways to settle disputes and laws to regulate the combatants during them. But make no mistake, conflict between the opposing groups still simmers and will flare from time to time. The manager may get along well with his employees. They may be on a first-name basis and truly enjoy sharing the plant's annual softball game and ox roast. But let a grievance become a strike and the attitude of both sides usually hardens to, "There's them and there's us." It's always been that way. Perhaps combativeness is instinctive to Americans. The tradition began a long time ago.

In the Spring of 1786, journeyman printers throughout New York City united to demand a guaranteed $1.00 minimum daily wage. Astounded employers immediately rejected the suggestion. The printers walked off their jobs. It was America's first organized labor strike. Except in those days it was called a "turnout." After several days of idle presses, the employers gave in. The "turnout" had been a success.

As the word spread, a series of "turnouts" occurred. Tailors, carpenters, weavers, coopers, gunsmiths, upholsterers, shoemakers. All "turnedout" for better wages—sometimes with "tramping committees," the first picket lines.

Employers, for the most part, gave in. They raised the wages. Then they waited. When the workers' skimpy alliances dissolved, they took back their raises and the whole process had to begin again. Except the workers were slow to learn about sticking together. It would take awhile.

It had taken them quite awhile to come this far. The need for workers— not English dandies but honest to gosh workers—had been there from the start. In 1609, Captain John Smith of Jamestown colony wrote his employers in England:

> "When you send again . . . rather send but thirty carpenters, husbandmen, gardeners, fishermen, masons, and diggers of tree roots, well provided, than a thousand such as we have."

Thousands risked the hazardous voyage and chancy future to come to America. Most were penniless. So they signed indentures, agreeing to serve the shipmaster (or a wealthy entrepeneur in England or in the Colonies) for five or more years. Others were convicted felons or refugees from debtors' prison, given the choice of jail or the Colonies.

In August, 1619 the Dutch ship "Treasurer" landed at Jamestown with a far more tragic ingredient to the labor mix—twenty strong negroes for sale as field hands. The Southern colonies were a little slow to adopt the idea. It was 1630 before a second ship, the "Fortune," brought more slaves. These were sold for "85 barrels of rum and 5 bushels of tobacco." This time the idea stuck. At a going price of only $400 per slave, and the black slave's ability to adjust to the harsh life of a field hand, it seemed a good investment. By 1860 there would be more than 4,000,000 black slaves throughout the South. It took Eli Whitney's cotton gin to slow the flood of slave immigrants; the Civil War to stop it for good.

So for several reasons, and usually with little money, immigrants came to America. There was plenty of work for them—land to be cleared and planted, towns and connecting roads to be built, creature comforts left behind in the Old Country to be made and sold.

Craftsmen owned their own shops. They used apprentices, usually bound for terms of five or six years and with no pay except food, clothing and shelter provided by the master as they learned his trade.

After our Revolutionary War, trademen moved to the frontiers. A distribution problem developed. There was need for warehouses, transport and capital investment. Enter jobbers, distributers, middlemen, merchant capitalists. Craftsmen no longer were free agents. Their goods—spinning wheels, furniture, plows, shoes, long rifles, knives, spun cloth—were held in warehouses, then in country stores. Quality gave way to quantity. Craftsmen were pushed; they pushed their workers.

"Sunup to sundown" was a phrase workers of the period understood very well. A Philadelphia shoemaker complained:

> " . . . no matter how hard I work . . . I earn only eight and one-half dollars a week . . . and I am at the bench from five in the morning until sunset. . . . "

As "push" turned to "shove," animosity developed between the master craftsmen and journeymen. Journeymen (skilled tradesmen who had completed an apprenticeship program) formed mutual protection associations—forerunners of the union. The common laborer, however, was excluded. It would be years before organized labor included laborers.

In 1792, Philadelphia shoemakers formed a permanent union with written constitution, dues and elected officers. It probably was the first local trade union in the United States. In 1794, New York printers set up a similar union. By 1804 trade unions or "societies" existed in most fields. They kept membership lists and activities secret, however, as employers blacklisted known members. Strikes or "turnouts," marked by great violence, followed. The term "scabs" was coined and much of the violence was aimed at those who worked while others struck.

Employers counterattacked in criminal courts. In March, 1806, eight Philadelphia shoemaker strikers were tried for "criminal conspiracy." The jury found them guilty and thereby established that it was illegal for workers to unite in any "society, association, union or club" for increased wages or other benefits. Between 1806 and 1840 there were numerous strikes (tailors in Baltimore; shipscarpenters in Philadelphia; cabinetmakers in Boston; glaziers and painters in New York City). Maimings, beatings, shootings and death punctuated most of them. All the while, unions remained illegal associations whose members could be tried in criminal court. It was not until 1842, when the Massachusetts Supreme Court ruled that they were not "conspiracies" and therefore not illegal, that "union" members began to come out in the open.

Meanwhile, the factory system developed and with it more reason for labor dissent. "Merchant capitalists" could not meet the demands of an exploding society. With New England's introduction of textile machinery came new production methods, a start at mass production. One man carded, another spun, a third wove, another pressed, and still another packed the product.

The new system increased production but aggravated labor-management conflict. And a new source of labor heaped fuel on the fire. Women and children joined the labor pool. Historians state that by 1820 more than half the factory workers in the United States were 9–10 years old. They worked an average of thirteen hours a day, six days a week, with about fifteen minutes for lunch. For all this, after the company deducted the cost of food and lodging in company dormitories, they earned between 33–67 cents per *week*. A nineteen year old girl described it:

"Oh, dear God, I wish to be dead. . . . I am enslaved in this dreadful place. There is no sweetness, no beauty, no joy . . . only clacking looms, whirring wheels, and clattering machinery. . . . Never a glimpse of blue sky, no dancing sunbeams, no sweet-smelling new-mown hay . . . this factory is an earthly hell. . . . "

At least one mill owner saw it another way:

"Hard work is good for the soul and a bulwark against Satan. We do not intend to let the Evil One capture the innocent girls in our charge."

An 1820s depression caused heavier demands on workers if they wanted to keep their jobs. An epidemic of strikes followed. Most were violent confrontations. The unions won some, lost some. All that seemed clear was that labor's hope for reforms lay in a united front. What still was not clear, however, was that the common laborers had to be enlisted too. The unions still offered membership only to craftsmen.

In 1827, Philadelphia city unions formed a central union council, called the "Mechanics Union of Trade Associations." It was the first city-wide labor organization. By 1836 thirteen other cities had formed similar associations. It was a start toward a national union.

In 1829, the Workingman's Party (a misnomer as only craftsmen were included) pressed for national labor reforms. Employers blackballed its members and livened its meetings with thugs, goons, strikebreakers, brawls. The party accomplished little and soon faded away.

If unions faltered, however, the country itself continued to grow. So did industry and commerce. Between 1830–1860 railroads spanned the continent. The value of manufactured goods leaped from $30 Million to $2 Billion. An immigrant flood drowned Eastern cities (about 300,000 of the 800,000 residents of New York City in 1860 were immigrants). Here were more cheap, unskilled laborers for farms and factories.

"Old hands," fresh off a boat themselves a few years before, resented newcomers. A pamphlet described the Irish, Germans and Swedes as:

" . . . sub-human beings . . . feeding upon the coarsest food . . . wearing the worst clothes . . . and having the habits of swine . . . not fit associates for American laborers and mechanics nor any decent members of society."

Labor thus spoke of the mote in management's eye, ignoring the beam in its own.

"Big Industry" welcomed new muscle to its factories. It had to; it needed it. In 1840 about 2,300,000 spindles operated in New England textile mills; by 1860 they had grown to more than 5,000,000 spindles. In

1830, 180,000 tons of iron ore were produced; by 1860 this had grown to 980,000 tons. By 1830 some 540 patents had been granted; by 1860 some 4,778 patents were recorded. Big industry had arrived.

Pennsylvania mills demanded more coal. Lots of it. West Virginia mine owners responded with more child labor, more hazardous mines. A New England mill owner expressed an accepted view of management's responsibility toward the worker:

> "So long as my hired hands do my work for what I choose to pay them, I keep them, getting out of them all I can. What they do or how they are outside my walls I don't know nor do I consider it to be my business to know. They must look out for themselves as I do for myself. When my machines get old and useless, I reject them and get new ones and these people are part of my machinery."

This kind of blunt language set the stage for the violent clashes which followed.

Workers felt enslaved, degraded, humiliated. They turned again to unions—larger ones. In 1852 journeymen printers (common laborers still excluded) formed the National Typographical Union. This was the first permanent national union. Similar unions for hat makers, cigar makers, iron moulders followed. Smaller unions, caught in a series of violent strikes and disputes, saw that big unions better held their own under fire. Growth of unions, however, was delayed by another conflict—our Civil War.

When it ended, in 1865, the South was destroyed. King Cotton was dead. Northern industrialists were in charge. Long live steel, meat, coal and oil, and the so-called "robber barons"—E. H. Harriman and Jay Gould (railroads), Andrew Carnegie (steel), John D. Rockefeller (oil). It was a time when success meant money, possessions, and never mind how one got them. Entrepeneurs, therefore, saw laborers as a commodity to be used.

Labor hoped that the National Labor Union (NLU), formed in 1866, would protect their rights. But the NLU attempted to do it by legislation. It didn't work; the entrepeneurs controlled the legislation. By 1872 the NLU had faded away. Labor now believed that reforms could be won only by force. They entered a new era of violence in labor-management relations.

On September 18, 1873, collapse of the banking firm of Jay Cooke triggered thousands of bankruptcies and seven years' depression. More than 4,000,000 Americans had no jobs. There were massive demonstrations.

One occurred on January 13, 1874. In Tompkins Square, New York City, an estimated crowd of 50,000 people gathered to hear speeches by reputedly radical union leaders. It all started peacefully enough and, as the speeches droned on, the crowd began to disperse. The Mayor had authorized the rally and policemen ringed the square. Suddenly, however, a police commander ordered, "Clear the square." The police immediately began to attack the crowd. Many people were hurt. In numerous other cities police prescribed the same dose for labor demonstrators. Newspapers labeled labor leaders as "foreign agitators who want to replace Old Glory with the red flag of anarchy."

Employers tried to cut wages. Workers fought back. Jay Gould, railroad magnate, suggested a solution: "I can hire one-half the working class to kill the other half."

Pennsylvania miners, realizing about $.50 per week after the company deducted for rent, food, clothing, formed the "Molly Maguires," a secret organization sometimes linked to the Ancient Order of Hibernians. The Molly Maguires struck back at tormenting mine company officials. Managers were beaten, bombed, shot. Companies fought back with private armies called "Coal and Iron Police."

Battles flared all over the Eastern coal fields. People were killed. The Allan Pinkerton Detective Agency hired out "industrial protection" detectives—goons, strikebreakers, labor spies. A Pinkerton detective, James McPharlan, joined the Ancient Order of Hibernians and the miners' union, the Workingmen's Benevolent Association. In 1875 he provided highly suspect evidence which led to the conviction for murder of twenty-four union leaders and miners. Ten were sentenced to death, the rest to long prison terms. It broke the strike—and the Workingmen's Benevolent Association.

On July 17, 1877, the Baltimore and Ohio Railroad cut crewmens' wages ten percent. Railroad crews at Martinsburg, West Virginia, walked off the job. Railroad telegraphers spread the word up the line. Within hours the Pennsylvania, New York Central, and Erie Railroads also were completely paralyzed. Railroad officials wired state capitals. State troops marched to Martinsburg. There was a scuffle, volley fire. Strikers were killed. Many more were wounded. Townspeople then fought militiamen.

The strike spread across the United States. When other state militias were called out, private citizens fought them. President Rutherford B. Hayes sent federal troops to stop demonstrations in Baltimore. An army officer commanded, "The order is to shoot to kill! These people are mutinous rabble, scurvy anarchists who deserve a bullet! I want them shot without mercy!" They were. In all, more than 100 people were killed, 300 wounded in armed clashes.

Labor unrest was not confined to the railroads. In 1869 a more promising and broader based labor union had been formed. Called the "Noble and Holy Order of the Knights of Labor (K of L), it was open to all workers, former workers, skilled and unskilled, men and women, white or black. Interestingly, it excluded only " . . . those who make their living by the sale of intoxicating drink . . . and lawyers, doctors, bankers."

Because of employers' blacklists and the violence attendant to union activity, the K of L practiced elaborate security measures, complete with passwords, codes, special handshakes. When meetings were scheduled, cryptic notices were chalked to nearby walls, somewhat like the hoboes' billboards of the 1930s.

In 1879, the K of L surfaced with 50,000 members. But they were restless, impatient members. The K of L leadership sought gradual social reforms, not strikes. And workers had been down that bumpy road too many times. When K of L Grand Master Workman Terence V. Powderly preached, "Longing for results, you have overlooked the fact that full and complete preparations have not yet been made," a labor paper replied, "No good general leads an army into battle without making ready . . . but it is not necessary for the last button to be sewn on the last private's overcoat. . . . "

In January, 1886, the K of L had 700,000 members. A small affiliate, the Federation of Organized Trades and Labor Unions, called for a national strike for the following May. On May 1 unions across the country struck. In Chicago more than 60,000 workers walked off their jobs. On May 3 workers rallied outside the McCormick Harvester Works, scene of a lockout. Fist fights began between company police and strikers. City police fired into the crowd. Six strikers were killed, twenty wounded.

The following evening several thousand citizens rallied in Haymarket Square, Chicago, to hear labor leaders denounce city and company officials. For more than four hours there was no violence. Then, with only 500 people remaining for the last speeches, a police Captain suddenly shouted, "I order you to disperse or take the consequences."

A bomb was thrown from the crowd. Gunfire was exchanged. When the smoke settled, seven policemen and four demonstrators were dead; about 200 more were wounded. The police charged eight of the speakers with murder. All were convicted. Five were sentenced to be hanged. One committed suicide in prison. The remaining four were executed. There were 250,000 marchers in the funeral procession and more than a quarter million spectators.

The Haymarket Square incident also killed the Knights of Labor. The American Federation of Labor (AF of L) rose from its ashes. Here was a different approach to labor-management relations: "We're not do-gooders, reformers, salvationists or bleeding hearts. We don't give a damn about anything except making a good living." The AF of L promised to seek labor gains "by negotiation if possible, by direct action if necessary. We don't want pie in the sky! We want it now! And we want as big a hunk of it as we can get!"

New AF of L leaders, unlike those of earlier labor groups, were not volunteers. They were paid, full-time employees. And many were very skilled. Unfortunately, many also were crooked, unscrupulous forerunners of more modern labor racketeers.

In July, 1892, the Amalgamated Association of Iron, Steel and Tin Workers, an affiliate of the AF of L, contested its contract with the Carnegie Steel Company. Carnegie was vacationing in Europe. His General Manager, Henry Clay Frick, locked out workers of the Homestead Works near Pittsburgh. He set up a high picket fence with barbed wire, firing slits, sentry boxes.

Workers dubbed it "Fort Frick," and 3,000 of them put it under siege. Frick then sent 300 Pinkerton "detectives," armed with Winchester repeating rifles, by barge up the Monongahela River to destroy the workers' lines. The workers, helped by townsmen, were ready. The Pinkerton barges never reached shore. For thirteen hours a fire fight of rifle fire and dynamite bombs raged. It ended when the workers poured oil on the river and set it afire. The invaders staggered ashore to be clubbed and beaten by the workers. Seven strikers and three Pinkerton men died in the melee. The governor then sent in 3,000 National Guardsmen. Frick followed up with 2,000 "scab" laborers. Then he wired Carnegie:

"Our victory is now complete. . . . I do not think we will ever have serious labor trouble again. . . . We had to teach our employees a lesson and we have taught them one they will never forget."

He was right. The strike was broken. So was the steel union. It would be forty years before the steel industry again was unionized. Carnegie responded, "Life is worth living again."

Two years later, Eugene V. Debs of the American Railway Union

(ARU) struck the Pullman Palace Car Company of Pullman, Illinois. Pullman was a typical "company town." Workers, charged for everything from food to rent to medical care, earned something like $6, after deductions, for two weeks' work. Debs' action caused another national railway strike. Twenty-four railroad companies banded to fight workers' demands. Federal troops intervened. A battalion of the 15th Infantry Regiment fought in Chicago streets. Thirty strikers were killed. Labor leaders were sentenced for inciting violence.

In 1902 the United Mine Workers (UMW) Union was active in West Virginia coal fields. They launched a strike. After six months, industries hurt for coal. And it was a cold December. President Theodore Roosevelt threatened to use federal troops to run the mines but, in the end, set up an arbitration committee that gave the UMW significant concessions.

A more colorful union, however, caught the public's eye. William "Big Bill" Haywood of the Western Federation of Miners had led a series of strikes characterized by mutual and frequent exchanges of rifle fire and dynamite bombs. No one was surprised as Haywood earlier had said:

> "I never yet saw a scab who didn't have a yellow streak up his back. . . . If you slug it out with him, toe-to-toe, you can bet your bottom dollar he'll take it on the lam. A working stiff has to fight or they'll make a doormat out of him."

In 1905 Haywood and others formed a new labor group: the Industrial Workers of the World (IWW). Called the "Wobblies," the preamble to their constitution made certain things clear:

> "The working class and the employing class have nothing in common. There can be no peace so long as hunger and want are found among millions of working people and the few who make up the employing class have all the good things of life. . . . "

It added, "It is the historic mission of the working class to do away with capitalism. . . . " The Wobblies welcomed all workers to their ranks. And many thousands signed on.

IWW organizer Joe Hill wrote songs that expressed their views. He fashioned his own words to popular ballads of the day. Like the one immortalizing a legendary Southern Pacific railroad engineer, Casey Jones, which Hill rewrote to his own purpose:

Casey Jones—the Union Scab
(Air: "Casey Jones)

The workers on the S.P. to strike sent out a call;
But Casey Jones the engineer, he wouldn't strike at all;
His boiler it was leaking, and its drivers on the bum,
And his engine and its bearings they were all out of plumb.

Chorus

Casey Jones kept his pink pile running;
Casey Jones was working double time;
Casey Jones got a wooden medal,
For being good and faithful on the S.P. Line.

Or, to the tune of "My Old Kentucky Home":

We Will Sing One Song

We will sing one song of the meek and humble slave,
The horn-handed son of the toil.
He's toiling hard from the cradle to the grave.
But his master reaps the profit from his toil.

———————

Then we'll sing one song of the greedy master class,
They're vagrants in broadcloth, indeed,
They live by robbing the ever-toiling mass,
Human blood they'll spill to satisfy their greed.

His "Little Red Songbook," a scarlet-covered pamphlet, fitted to the size of an overall pocket. His songs became national favorites. So did the IWW.

The union, however, was short-lived. Convicted of murder, Joe Hill was executed by firing squad in Utah. His last words were, "Don't mourn! Organize!"

Haywood and other IWW leaders were tried for the bomb assassination of a former governor of Idaho. Renowned criminal lawyer, Clarence Darrow, won an acquittal, and the IWW continued to meet violence with violence. They began many strikes: won some, lost some. But in 1917, when Haywood and ninety-six other Wobbly leaders denounced America's entry into World War I, IWW leaders were jailed for anti-war pronouncements. Haywood skipped bail to flee to Russia where he died in 1928 and was buried in the Kremlin.

Without its leaders, the IWW movement faded away. Only its songs lingered, to appear again in future labor struggles.

In 1914, President Woodrow Wilson pressed Congress for pro-labor legislation. It responded with the Clayton Act. This law stated that labor unions were not in restraint of trade, nor were they "conspiracies." Congress then created the Department of Labor with the Secretary of Labor a Cabinet member.

Labor now had a legal voice at court. Union membership grew. World War I brought a feeling of national unity but, while living costs soared, wages did not. In 1917, more than 1,000,000 workers participated in nearly 5,000 strikes. Wilson responded with a War Labor Board, consisting of management and labor representatives. Both made concessions. Labor gained much it had sought. War production escalated.

The era of good feelings didn't last. With the Armistice, government controls were lifted. Employers tried to cut workers' benefits. Labor struck. During 1919–1920, more than 1,000,000 workers tramped picket lines. Steel workers struck the US Steel Corporation in Pittsburgh. The strike began on September 22, 1919 and was not crushed until January, 1920 after violent clashes between strikers and company police with individuals clubbed, trampled, shot.

Within a few years, however, great national prosperity eased labor-management pressures. Labor was making money. More money than ever before. So, they argued, why rock the boat? Labor's militancy eased. And they forgot to keep their own skirts clean. Gangsters and racketeers infiltrated labor unions. Some corporations tried to take back earlier concessions. They sought "yellow dog" contracts, preventing new employees from joining unions and lobbied for "open shops" by which union and non-union men could be hired. Unions resisted but, so long as there was some money to be made, not with the militancy of the past.

That ended in 1929 with the collapse of the stock market and the Depression that followed. By 1932, 14,000,000 Americans were out of work. Breadlines were common. There was little hope. The people shouted, "We want jobs," but neither government nor industry could find them. Not yet. Eventually, President Franklin D. Roosevelt led the nation out of the Depression.

Legislation during Roosevelt's administration was designed to put people back to work. It included the National Industrial Recovery Act (NRA) which stimulated business. The NRA also established minimum wages and hours codes and assured workers the right to organize and to bargain collectively without employers' interference. This was followed (1935) by the National Labor Relations Act (called the Wagner Act), which specifically banned labor spies, blacklists, forcing of "yellow dog" contracts, actions that coerced or restrained union activity.

From 1935 on, under the aegis of the Wagner Act, there were savage confrontations along the labor front as both sides tested provisions of the Act. A labor historian reports that more than 2500 corporations employed labor spies and cited one steel company as girding up its loins at one plant with 8 machine guns, 369 rifles, 190 shotguns, 450 revolvers, 6,000 rounds of ammunition, 109 gas guns and 3,000 tear gas shells.

John L. Lewis, mine workers' leader, broke from the AF of L to form the Congress of Industrial Organizations (CIO). For the first time an intensive effort was made to organize all uncommitted workers. Thousands rallied to the CIO banner. That led to another tragic encounter.

The CIO struck Republic Steel. On Sunday, May 30, 1937, striking workers held a union picnic/rally near the Republic Steel's South Chicago mill. Police and special deputies armed with weapons, grenades, clubs, attacked the group. In the fight, which the Union tagged "the Memorial Day Massacre," ten strikers were killed, many wounded. That ended the strike but ushered in a return to violence.

Labor conflict flared periodically into the 1940s. Except for a few brief wildcat strikes, however, during World War II there were few clashes.

After the war, a wave of strikes for increased worker benefits occurred. Now unions had trained leaders and ample pocketbooks. By 1946 they'd won ample gains. They'd also found themselves infested with racketeers who'd worked their way into union management positions.

Because of union power abuses and the presence of unsavory individuals in union leadership positions, Congress passed the Taft-Hartley Bill (1947), limiting certain powers of the unions and requiring stricter government control over union activities. Although the Act did not please labor, it eased conflict between the AF of L and the CIO and regulated the conduct of disputes between labor and management. In 1955, the AF of L and the CIO merged a membership of 15,000,000 men and women.

Since that time unions have continued to win employee benefits from management. When negotiation has failed, strikes have occurred. Some have been relatively quiet and peaceful; some have been marked by violence and prolonged bitterness. But both sides have been forced to conform their activities to restrictions provided by laws.

Strikes occur. Picket lines appear. A season of "testing" follows. Sometimes this includes violence or other unfair or illegal labor practices, as defined by the law. When this happens, courts order restraint. Usually, to a greater or less degree, it works. Eventually the disputes are resolved.

It is during the contest itself, before the disputes are resolved, that the Security Director must practice his art. His mission is to be neutral, a referee to be trusted and respected by both sides. He is not involved with negotiations to end the conflict. That is another's responsibility. His is to prevent violence and illegal acts toward individuals or to property.

The more he understands the long and bumpy road labor and management have traveled in their relationship toward one another, the better his chance of saying, "Keep it clean, gentlemen," and making that ruling stick.

CHAPTER 2

INDUSTRIAL RELATIONS

This text suggests means by which a company can improve its security during labor-management crises. That means less violence, less chance of people getting hurt, less chance of property (company and private) being damaged. By reducing flashpoints it also may mean differences resolved faster and with less bad feeling, hence people back on the job a lot quicker and happier to be there.

Although the text focuses on industrial strikes, where security problems probably are more intense, cited concepts and techniques apply to any working environment.

The better the Security Director knows industrial relations, collective bargaining processes, and the functions, responsibilities, personalities of labor and management for his company, the better equipped he is to keep the peace between the two groups. And that is a big part of his job.

Incidentally, only masculine pronouns are used in the text. This is not to favor men nor to ignore or denegrate women. There is room for both in the security field. But it simplifies things to avoid the "he/she" problem. Let the reader adjust as he/she wishes.

We have traced the history of the American labor movement, a good start toward understanding the nature of the problem. This chapter defines terms frequently used in industrial relations. The next one highlights pertinent labor laws. With that background in hand, we can consider specifics of strike management.

Some consider "industrial relations" to be all that happens from the time an individual applies for a job until he leaves it: recruiting, hiring, training, assigning, promoting, disciplining, job benefits, termination or retirement. Others limit the term to labor-management relations. Although the more the Security Director knows about the broader "industrial relations" the better, we'll limit the term to the handling of labor-management crises—strikes.

The term "Security Director" is meant to be the individual who is responsible for the security of his company. That may be his sole mission.

In larger corporations it usually is that way. It may be, however, that security is only one of several hats worn by that individual. Security may be only an additional duty for someone primarily responsible for personnel, training, safety or industrial relations. Whatever other assignments he may have, if he is responsible for the company's security problems, he is the man we'll refer to as the "Security Director."

The term "management" applies to an employer or to executives of a corporation who are responsible for the administration, operation, direction of that corporation and for exercising leadership within it.

"Labor" refers to work—human work—to produce and distribute goods or services for which some compensation is expected. When a group of workers voluntarily combine in an association to improve their pay, work hours, working conditions, their association is called a "union." Their group activity becomes part of "the labor movement."

The "local union," or "Local," is the basic unit of the labor organization. The rifle company, if you will, of labor's army. The term generally applies to the labor organization of a single plant or a small geographical area. A Local may represent a single company or plant. Crafts unions, on the other hand, such as plumbers, carpenters, electricians may include several companies within a region.

National unions, such as the American Federation of Labor-Congress of Industrial Organizations or the International Brotherhood of Teamsters, or the Chauffeurs, Warehousemen and Helpers of America, merge many local unions within an industry or craft. Still other unions, called "independent unions," are organized within a single plant or company and have no national affiliation.

Just as management has its hierarchy, so do unions. Individuals who have responsibility for guiding and administering union programs and for providing leadership to their unions are referred to as "union leadership."

The "Union Steward," or "Shop Steward," is the individual responsible for union activities, usually at the department level. Usually elected by his fellow union members, he attempts to handle grievances (employees' complaints against any facet of their employment) in their earliest stage, collects dues, disseminates union information, and generally represents the union at the lowest working level. Assisting him may be a small group of workers, elected on a shift-wide basis, called a "Shop Committee." The Chief Steward heads the Shop Stewards, coordinates union activity throughout the plant and represents the union in dealing with higher management.

The general term "Union Membership" applies to all who are members of a union. Privates in the ranks, the working people, are called the "rank and file."

A "Closed Shop" is a union security agreement in which the employer has agreed to hire or continue to employ only employees who are members of the union. The Closed Shop is illegal under federal labor statutes.

A "Union Shop" is a form of union security in which the employer contracts to require all new employees to become members of that company's union and to remain a member *or* to pay union dues during the current contract. The US Supreme Court has ruled that the Union Shop is legal under Section 8 of the Taft-Hartley Act but that individual states have authority to outlaw them. Many have.

A plant or company without a union, or one in which no union has been designated as the "Collective Bargaining Agent," is called a "Non-Union Shop."

"Collective Bargaining" is the process of negotiating terms and conditions of employment and establishing procedures for interpreting and administering the resulting "contract" (written agreement). The process is carried on between management and the employees' collective bargaining agent. This is the union officially certified by the National Labor Relations Board or a state labor agency as the exclusive bargaining agent for all employees (union and non-union) of that bargaining unit.

The contract probably specifies "plant rules," general working rules of an establishment. Management normally enforces these rules by various punitive measures short of discharge. For serious violations, of course, employees may be discharged.

The contract also may specify rules or procedures for handling "grievances," complaints by any employee, by the union, or by management, concerning any part of the employment relationship.

"Grievance Committees," groups of labor-management representatives, attempt to resolve grievances at the lowest level possible. Sometimes settlement seems impossible. The grievance then may become a "dispute," a significant controversy between employer and union, or perhaps within the union, which leads to "job actions."

"Job actions," sometimes called "direct actions," are union tactics which skirt or ignore the collective bargaining machinery established by an existing contract. They may be threats, work slowdowns, strikes.

The Constitution of the United States gives workmen the right to refuse to work under conditions believed to be unfair. These same freedoms give the employer the right to conduct his business, to protect his property, to defend his employment policies and work standards. These conflicting rights can and often do lead to violent disagreement between the two sides.

A "strike" has been defined as:

> "A temporary stoppage of work or a concerted withdrawal from work by a group of employees to express a grievance or to enforce demands affecting wages, hours or working conditions."

It is "concerted" because it involves a number of workers; it is "temporary" because the employees expect to return to work once their dispute is resolved.

The "right to strike" is a phrase often heard in labor relations. Its meaning is not quite clear, but generally it is associated with an employee's right to stop working for his employer.

There is no *unqualified* right to strike. Strikes to support *lawful* labor objectives are protected by the US Constitution but in each instance the question is whether the objectives of a particular strike are *lawful.* That depends on current legislation and the courts and the National Labor Relations Board's (NLRB) interpretation of them in terms of the dispute in question.

As a general rule, strikes are illegal when called for an illegal purpose or when conducted in an unlawful manner. The following type strikes, for example, may be unlawful:

a. "Sit-down strikes" where employees stop work but remain at the job site and refuse to leave the company premises.

b. Strikes accompanied by violence. These become unlawful even when begun for a lawful purpose.

c. Strikes in violation of "required notice" provisions of federal law. Economic strikes (inability of employer and employees to agree on wages, hours, working conditions), for example, must be preceded by at least a sixty-day notice to employers, thirty days' notice to federal and state agencies, that the union wishes to modify the existing collective bargaining agreement when it expires. This "sixty-day notice" does not mean that a strike must follow. A strike in the absence of such notice, however, would be illegal.

d. Strikes in violation of federal statutes such as by unions or groups not "certified" by the NLRB as the official and exclusive bargaining agent for its local; jurisdictional strikes where several unions vie for the right to represent the workers or to perform certain services; strikes involving "hot cargoes" wherein unions demand that their employers not handle shipments by other employers which unions consider to be unfair (goods bearing no union label, for example, or goods produced by employers believed to be substandard in pay or working conditions for their employees); certain secondary strikes or boycotts (strikes to pressure companies not involved in a basic labor dispute but who have dealings with the primary company).

e. Strikes in violation of a valid no-strike clause in the existing contract. These are also known as "wildcat strikes."

The common variety of strike involves the presence of a labor organization. Employees, however, may strike when there is no union involved in any way. A strike in a non-union facility may be legally protected by federal labor laws if it is in protest of wages, hours or working conditions and of mutual interest to all employees.

Because of the complexity of laws in this field it is critically important that managers and especially Security Directors (who will be right in the trenches in any strike) coordinate planned actions with a labor lawyer during any work stoppage or strike situation, whether a union is involved or not, until the dispute is resolved. For example, if the employer is proven to be involved in an "unfair labor practice," as defined by federal or state statutes and interpreted by the courts, the union has a right, without a sixty-day warning, to strike to force correction of those "unfair labor practices." Further, if a strike properly can be classified as an unfair labor practice strike, all striking employees who unconditionally request to return to their jobs, with the possible exception of those engaged in violent or criminal conduct, must be allowed to do so. Even if the employer has hired replacements for them.

During a strike employer and union are required to engage in "good faith bargaining" (reasonable and sincere efforts) to resolve the dispute. A third party intermediary often helps. "Negotiators" (persons responsible to the union or to management to represent their group), unable to resolve basic differences between the two parties, may be helped in the "conciliation" process by an impartial third party "mediator" who not only acts as a go-between but also suggests possible avenues for resolving a particular issue in dispute.

While collective bargaining negotiations continue, each side will do what it can away from the bargaining table to improve its position. The most common union tactic to demonstrate its strength and resolve is "picketing." Picketing is patrolling by strikers, at or near the employer's place of business to give notice that a labor dispute is in progress, to persuade workers to join the union's lines, or to discourage or prevent persons from entering the struck facility, particularly those entering it to work.

Picketing serves a variety of purposes and may take many forms. Mass picketing involves patrolling, frequently with placards or banners, plant entrances or the front of a store or facility which presumably is unfair to the union. When it involves a column of workers who, by locking arms or walking in close file, prevent persons or vehicles from passing through the picket lines, it is called "Chain Picketing" and is illegal.

"Dry-run picketing" is a tactic used without a formal strike (during negotiations, in organizing union activity at the facility, etc.) to bring pressure on management and to show union strength.

"Peaceful picketing" is a term given to picketing ostensibly to show that a labor dispute is in progress or that a firm purchases or uses non-union material or services. Whether the picketing is "peaceful" or not depends on whether there is violence or whether pickets threaten those who wish to cross their lines. Both situations may be very difficult to define. As one Justice observed in a railroad labor dispute, "There is and can be no such thing as peaceful picketing, any more than there can be chaste vulgarity, or peaceful mobbing, or lawful lynching."

An employer can retaliate by a "lockout." This is his form of economic pressure. He shuts down the struck facility so that even if union members wish to work they cannot. Lockouts and strikes may be tough birds to identify. Provocation by the employer often is difficult to prove. The union argues that management locked its members from their work place; management answers, "Not so," and calls it a strike. The public usually sees only picket lines and picket signs and is more apt to believe "strike" than "lockout."

The danger now is in confrontations, particularly during the first seventy-two hours of a strike or other job action. That is when union strength peaks, the juices on both sides flow freely, neither side is sure what it should or should not do. Tactical mistakes in unusual situations, angry or obscene words or gestures, or unnecessary confrontations, often lead to violence. Once uncapped, that particular genie is hard to cram back into its bottle. And it may set the tone for the remainder of the strike.

Whichever side can prove it has been dealt with in an unfair or illegal manner may win relief through state or federal courts. This comes in the form of an "injunction," a prohibitory order issued by a court to restrain an individual or group from committing an act that the court regards as unfair to some other person concerned.

The Norris-LaGuardia Act (1932) forbade federal courts from issuing injunctions in labor disputes unless certain prior conditions were fulfilled. This is discussed in the next chapter, but it includes allowing the other party to present its case, assuring that all other methods to resolve the issue have failed, and proving that witholding the injunction would cause more harm to one party than granting it would cause to the other.

The Taft-Hartley Act and the Landrum-Griffin Act which followed cited three instances where an injunction would be appropriate:

a. Restraining a person from committing an alleged unfair labor practice.

b. Restraining an alleged unfair labor practice as in a secondary boycott or recognition picketing (picketing whose primary purpose is to pressure the employer into allowing that union to be the employees' exclusive bargaining agent).

c. Restraining a strike involving a national emergency.

The injunction may be a temporary restraint or a permanent prohibition of the act in question. For example, it may *limit* a certain labor leader's participation in a certain strike to particular activities or it may *bar* him from all participation in it.

A "Blanket Injunction" is a court order so broad in its prohibitions that it includes activities which have little apparent relation to the dispute in question. Management would welcome a blanket injunction as it could severely limit union tactics; the union, of course, would oppose it.

The NLRB or appropriate state agency may order an employer or union to stop what it has determined to be an unfair labor practice by a "Cease and Desist Order."

Hopefully, the security staff, in coordination with management and union officials, will be able to prevent violence and other illegal activities calling for court involvement. The more successful they are, the better the chance for early resolution of the dispute with minimum bad feelings on both sides.

In this chapter we have considered terms most frequently found in labor disputes. The "definitions" have been sketchy and general in tone. At the end of the text is a more comprehensive glossary. It too, however, only points the reader in the right general direction. For further information and other terms, I suggest *Roberts's Dictionary of Industrial Relations* by Harold S. Roberts, BNA Incorporated, Washington, DC, 1966, or a similar text.

Please note the quotation from Mr. Justice Holmes at the start of the glossary. Words cannot safely be taken out of context. Sometimes they are difficult to define, harder to understand, harder still to apply properly. Industrial relations is a complex and difficult field. In handling a strike situation, management (and especially the Security Director) should work very closely with the company's legal representative so that their activities always are within the intent of the law and so that they may be alert to detect and quickly stop unfair or illegal labor practices by the union or by their own staffs.

Overall strike management operations may be the basic responsibility of the struck company's operating and legal staffs but unless their actions are timely, effective and legal the Security Director may find that he's the one who must live with their failings, on the picket line.

CHAPTER 3

LABOR LAWS

Congress and the state legislatures have enacted a series of laws regulating relations between labor and management. Earlier laws seem designed to protect workers and unions from excesses by management. More recent laws, however, have been concerned with union excesses; the presence of labor racketeers and mobsters in union ranks; union leaders who have lined their own pockets with union funds.

These labor laws are complex by nature because, like all laws, they are subject to interpretation. What is "unfair"? What is "improper"? Who really threw the first stone? Courts must consider the intent of the law then judge whether a management or union complaint is valid and warrants sanctions on the other party.

The Security Director who is trying to keep the peace in a labor dispute must use his resources in a legal and proper manner. He also must advise other managers of security aspects of their use of other company resources. Most important, he is the management representative nearest the picket lines, nearest the action. He must recognize illegal acts and document them. In all this it helps if he has a reasonable idea of federal and state labor laws which may apply to his situation.

This chapter highlights the more prominent federal labor laws. The discussion is general and in no way will make the reader an expert on labor laws. For further information and for specific guidance in a strike situation, the Security Director should confer with the company's legal representative.

Sherman Act

The Sherman Act (Anti-Trust Act of 1890) was directed toward industry's monopolistic practices, combinations of increasingly larger and more powerful firms (steel, oil, railroads, etc.) which squeezed out smaller competitors. In practice, however, it also was applied to labor unions and this led to the Clayton Act of 1914.

The Sherman Act's chief concerns were expressed as follows:

"Every contract, combination in the form of trust or otherwise, or conspiracy, in restraint of trade or commerce among the several States . . . is hereby declared illegal. . . .

"Every person who shall make any such contract or engage in any such combination or conspiracy hereby declared to be illegal shall be deemed guilty of a misdemeanor . . . and . . . shall be punished by fine not exceeding fifty thousand dollars, or by imprisonment not exceeding one year, or by both. . . . "

Clayton Act

The Clayton Act (Anti-Trust Act of 1914) was meant to bar applying the Sherman Act's provisions to combinations of labor (unions) and to limit courts' jurisdiction to issue injunctions in labor disputes. Critical extracts follow:

"Section 6.   That the labor of a human is not a commodity or article of commerce. Nothing in the anti-trust laws shall be construed to forbid the existence and operation of labor . . . organizations, instituted for the purpose of mutual help . . . or to forbid or restrain individual members of such organizations from lawfully carrying out the objectives thereof, nor shall such organizations, or the members thereof, be held or construed to be illegal combinations or conspiracies in restraint of trade. . . .

"Section 20.   That no restraining order or injunction shall be granted by any court in the United States . . . and in any case between an employer and employees . . . involving or growing out of a dispute concerning terms or conditions of employment, unless necessary to prevent irreparable injury to property, or to a property right . . . for which injury there is no adequate remedy at law. . . . "

The law was hailed as labor's "Magna Charta." Subsequent judicial interpretation, however, indicated that something more was needed. This led to the Norris-LaGuardia Act (1932) and the Wagner-Connery Act (1935).

Railway Labor Act

This law, passed in 1926, was based on a joint labor-management proposal to resolve railroad labor disputes by mediation and voluntary arbitration (willingness by both parties to be bound by the decision of a mutually acceptable third party). In 1934 the Act was extended to cover the airlines' industry.

The law protected employees' right to organize and to bargain collectively. Contracts had to be filed with a created National Mediation Board which also was charged with certifying the union to represent employees and with mediating disputes. The law also established a National Railroad Adjustment Board to resolve grievances arising from alleged violations of existing contracts.

Norris-LaGuardia Act

The Norris-LaGuardia Act (Anti-Injunction Act of 1932) declared it public policy to protect workers' freedom of association and collective bargaining:

> "... it is necessary that the [worker] have full freedom of association, self organization, and designation of representatives of his own choosing, to negotiate the terms and conditions of his employment, and that he shall be free from interference, restraint or coercion of employers of labor, or their agents, in the designation of such representatives or in self-organization or in other concerted activities for the purpose of collective bargaining or other mutual aid or protection...."

The law declared "yellow dog" contracts illegal. These provided that, as a condition of employment, the worker agrees not to join a union and, if presently a union member, to resign that membership.

The law also declared that a union officer was not responsible for acts committed during a labor dispute unless he specifically authorized those acts. It further provided for trial by jury for individuals charged with contempt of court in a labor dispute.

It limited the use of injunctions in labor disputes:

> "No court in the United States ... shall ... issue any restraining order or temporary or permanent injunction in a case involving or growing out of a labor dispute, except in strict conformity with the provisions of this Act; nor shall any such restraining order or temporary or permanent injunction be issued contrary to the public policy declared in this Act."

Specifically, the law allowed workers to strike, to picket, to engage in primary and secondary boycotting, and to engage in related activities. It cited nine specific activities as protected from court injunctions:

    a. Concerted stoppage or refusal to work.

    b. Joining or remaining a union member.

c. Providing financial help to persons participating in or interested in a labor dispute and involved in litigation.

d. Publicizing the existence of a dispute by any method not involving fraud or violence.

e. Assembling peaceably to promote the interests of participants in a labor dispute.

f. Notifying anyone of an intent to pursue activities cited above (a–e).

g. Agreeing with others to do or not to do these activities cited above (a–e).

Further, courts could not issue an injunction unless it was proved that:

a. Unlawful acts had been committed or are threatened.

b. Irreparable injury to property has been committed or is imminent.

c. The petitioner has more to lose if the injunction is refused than will be suffered by employees or union if it is granted.

d. The petitioner has no adequate remedy at law.

e. The police are unable or unwilling to protect the petitioner's property.

National Industrial Recovery Act

The National Industrial Recovery Act of 1933 meant to help industry police itself by establishing codes to eliminate unfair competitive practices and to protect employers under the Sherman Act of 1890. The codes also established procedures for determining minimum wages and maximum work hours.

The law also protected the right of employees to organize and thus helped union organizing efforts during the early days of the Roosevelt Administration.

In 1935 the U.S. Supreme Court declared the law unconstitutional.

Copeland Act

The Copeland Act (Anti-Kickback Law of 1934) was designed to stop federally-financed projects employers' requiring their workers to return part of their pay as a condition of employment. It also barred all employers from using force, threats, or other means of coercion to require an employee to return part of his pay to keep his job.

Hobbs Act

The Hobbs Act (Anti-Racketeering Act of 1934) forbade the use of extortion, force or violence in interstate commerce. It made it illegal for unscrupulous labor unions to blackmail employers, as in "featherbedding," a practice by which unions made work for their members through limiting production or the amount of work to be performed or by make-work arrangements, or to accept bribes for not calling strikes.

Wagner-Connery Act

The Wagner-Connery Act (National Labor Relations Act—NLRA) was passed by the Congress in 1935, a short time after the US Supreme Court declared the National Industrial Recovery Act unconstitutional.

It was designed to stimulate the economy by removing prohibitions of anti-trust laws and allowing businesses to organize and control prices.

Perhaps the heart of the law is its Section 7 which guarantees:

"Employees shall have the right to self-organization, to form, join, or assist labor organizations, to bargain collectively through representatives of their own choosing, and to engage in concerted activities, for the purpose of collective bargaining, or other mutual aid or protection."

It cited specific employer unfair labor practices:

a. Interfering with, restraining, or coercing employees in the exercise of rights guaranteed in Section 7.

b. Dominating or interfering with the formation or administration of any labor organization or contributing financial or other support to it.

c. Discriminating in hiring, length of employment or any other term or condition of employment either to encourage or discourage membership in a union. This proviso was modified, however, to allow employers to contract with unions to require, as a condition of employment, that employees become members of the union certified as representing that company's employees. This provision subsequently was modified by the Taft-Hartley Act which banned closed shops and permitted individual states to enact "right to work" legislation by which an employee need not join the union so long as he agreed to pay its dues and other assessments as a "service charge" for the union's representing his interests.

d. Discharging or otherwise discriminating against an employee because he has filed charges or testified under the National Labor Relations Act.

e. Refusing to bargain collectively with the employees' union.

The law set forth the principle of majority rule in selecting the union to represent all employees with final certification by the NLRB which also is charged with "preventing any person from engaging in any unfair labor practice." During the twelve year period in which the Wagner-Connery Act was in effect, more than 100,000 cases of alleged unfair labor practices and employee representation complaints resulted.

Finally, the law stated that "Nothing in this Act shall be construed so as to interfere with or impede or diminish in any way the right to strike."

The most common complaint against the Wagner-Connery Act was that it favored labor unions. Critics charged that although employers were required to respect the statutory rights of workers, the workers were immune to any like restrictions for indiscriminate picketing, boycotts, strikes or conduct at the bargaining table.

The Taft-Hartley Act of 1947 would attempt to rectify this alleged imbalance of power and responsibility.

Byrnes Act

The Byrnes Act (Anti-Strikebreaking Act of 1936) intended to prevent employers' transporting strikebreakers across state lines. A strikebreaker is a person, not a regular employee, who accepts employment in a struck plant (distinguished from a "scab," who already is an employee but who continues working during a strike). The strikebreaker may work, or may be a guard, or simply be a professional strikebreaker.

The Act was amended in 1938 to limit itself to individuals whose sole purpose is to interfere with peaceful picketing.

Fair Labor Standards Act of 1938

This law attempted to regulate healthful working conditions, minimum wages, overtime pay, and child labor in the production of goods for interstate commerce. It has been amended seven times and has complicated coverage and exceptions. It is of interest as it concerns general coverage of employees but probably would not involve the Security Director except during demonstrations or other job actions related to "hot cargo" disputes (cargoes allegedly produced or shipped in violation of the provisions of the Fair Labor Standards Act).

Hatch Act

The Hatch Act (Federal Corrupt Practices Act of 1947) makes it unlawful for any labor organization to make a contribution or expenditure supporting the political candidacy of any Presidential or Vice Presidential electors, a Senator or Representative, or a Delegate or Resident Commissioner to Congress.

The Constitutionality of the law has not been tested. In two rulings it was decided that payment of union general funds to cover the cost of publishing a specific issue of a union newspaper which contained the union's endorsement of a particular candidate was not illegal as the paper was published regularly anyway, but that payment for a specific one-time political broadcast supporting Congressional candidates was improper.

Taft-Hartley Act

The Taft-Hartley Act (Labor-Management Relations Act of 1947) certainly has been the most controversial, most union-opposed bill in the history of US labor legislation. The bill was vetoed by President Harry S. Truman with his affirmation that it would "reverse the basic direction of our national labor policy." The Congress, however, overrode his veto and it became law.

During World War II unions had "grown like Topsy," from 5,000,000 members in 1940 to about 15,000,000 in 1945. In 1945 a great wave of strikes involved nearly 5,000,000 workers and nearly every major industry. More than 38,000,000 man-days of labor were lost. Many saw the strikes as an arrogant display of union power. They resented it. News media demanded reforms to the Wagner-Connery Act. The public agreed.

The strikes increased in 1946: more than 1,000,000,000 man-days' labor lost. Strikes among coal mines and utility companies threatened public health and safety. President Truman threatened to draft rail strikers. Some so-called "labor leaders" were little more than racketeers. When peaceful picketing failed, strikes and picketing became violent. There were union abuses in admitting new members, in kickback extortions, in exhorbitant fees. Closed shop unions abused workers' right to organize and to bargain collectively. Defense contracts were delayed while unions fought. Secondary boycotts became a powerful union weapon. Teamsters could paralyze any business dependent upon trucking. A house cleaning was needed; the public clamored for it.

In introducing the bill, co-author Senator Robert A. Taft declared that:

> "Supreme Court interpretations of the Norris-LaGuardia Anti-Injunction Act and the Clayton Act seem to have placed union activities, no matter how destructive to the rights of the individual workers and employers who are conforming to the National Labor Relations Act, beyond the pale of Federal law."

Co-author Fred Hartley added:

> "For the last fourteen years, as a result of labor laws ill-conceived and disastrously executed, the American working man has been deprived of his dignity as an individual. He has been cajoled, coerced, intimidated, and on many occasions beaten up.... He has ... had to pay them tribute to get a job. He has been forced into labor organizations against his will. At other times when he has desired to join a particular labor organization he has been prevented from doing so and forced to join another one. He has been compelled to contribute to causes and candidates for public office to which he was opposed. He has been prohibited from expressing his own mind on public issues. He has been denied any voice in arranging the terms of his own employment. He has frequently, against his own will, been called out on strikes....
>
> "The employer's plight has likewise not been happy. He has witnessed the productive capacity of his plants sink to alarmingly low levels. He has been required to employ or reinstate individuals who have destroyed his property and assaulted other employees.... He has seen the loyalty of his supervisors undermined by compulsory unionism.... He has been compelled to bargain with the same union that bargains with his competitors and thus to reveal to his competitors the secrets of his business. He has had to stand helplessly by while employees desiring to enter his plant to work have been obstructed by violence, mass picketing, and general rowdyism.... His business ... has been virtually brought to a standstill by disputes over which he himself was not a party...."

The Taft-Hartley Act is broader in scope than the earlier Wagner-Connery Act (NLRA) and considerably revises it.

It preserves the rights of workers to organize and to bargain collectively but imposes on both sides the requirement to bargain in good faith.

It cites specific employers' activities to be considered unfair labor practices. It also outlaws concerted union pressure by violence, intimidation, certain types of secondary boycotts.

It revives use of labor injunctions as a relief against unfair labor practices but avoids restrictions imposed by the earlier Norris-LaGuardia Act. It bans closed shop union security, permits only a form of the union shop (contract requiring membership in the certified union *or* payment of union fees by employees not wishing to join the union itself) while allowing individual states to mandate open shops by "right to work" laws.

It continues the NLRB and also establishes the Federal Mediation and Conciliation Service as an independent agency to help resolve labor disputes where the collective bargaining process has failed.

Perhaps most important, it authorizes suits of labor organizations in federal courts and excludes supervisory personnel, including foremen, from the protection of the law. Employers therefore need not recognize or bargain collectively with supervisory employees. Both provisions put powerful weapons in management's hands.

More specifically, Section 7 of the Taft-Hartley Act repeats guarantees of employees' rights to organize and to bargain collectively but amends a portion of the Wagner-Connery Act by now giving employees the right to refrain from joining a union and engaging in concerted activities, except when the union and employer have agreed to a union-shop security clause. In these cases, where the Wagner Act required them to join the union, they now could refuse to join so long as they paid union assessments as a "fee for services." Employees had the right to strike but they also now had the right *not* to strike, to go on working, if they wished, despite a union strike.

Section 8 lists *employer* unfair labor practices:

a. Interfering with, restraining or coercing employees in exercising their rights. For example: questioning employees about their union activity or membership so as to cause fear; spying on union meetings; threatening loss of jobs or benefits for union membership; granting wage increases timed to discourage employees' joining a union; disciplining employees for complaining about wages or working conditions, even if no union is involved.

b. Dominating or interfering with the formation or administration of a union or contributing financial or other support to it; pressuring employees to join a union (except when under a union-security contract); allowing several unions to compete on company property and during working hours for the right to represent employees but denying that right to other unions; recognizing, negotiating, or signing a contract with a union not certified to represent a majority of the employees (exceptions in the garment and construction industries); expanding a union's "coverage" to a new company facility without vote by the employees in that new facility.

(c) Discriminating against an employee because he belongs to a union or because he chooses not to belong to the union certified to represent the firm's employees but has agreed to pay union assessed charges. The employer cannot fire employees in a *lawful* strike but he can permanently replace them. If the striker wishes to return to work and his position has been filled, he must be given preference in filling another vacancy for which he is qualified. Employers can fire employees for striking in violation of a "no-strike" clause; striking to further an unfair labor practice by the union; striking to amend a contract without complying with required strike warnings; committing violence during a strike. Any employee, union or non-union, may be fired for just cause at any time.

The same section cites unfair labor practices by the *union:*

a. Restraining or denying employees' rights to form or join labor organizations of their own choice. To a certain extent, however, unions can adopt and enforce internal rules governing its members, such as fining a member for not attending regular union meetings or for working during a lawful strike.

b. Causing or attempting to cause an employer or the union itself to discriminate against an employee, as in forcing an employee to join a union or to participate in union-sanctioned activities.

c. Refusing to bargain collectively with an employer.

d. Engaging in a strike or encouraging employees to engage in a strike to force an employer to recognize or bargain with a union not certified as representing its employees.

e. Forcing an employer to join any labor organization in refusing to do business with another employer (secondary boycott). Individual employees, however, could refuse to enter the premises of another employer whose employees are on lawful strike.

f. Forcing an employer to assign particular work to employees of one labor organization in preference to another or permitting a "seniority" work arrangement within their own union.

g. Requiring excessive payments for employees to become a member of the union.

h. Causing or attempting to cause an employer to pay for services not performed (featherbedding).

Subsequent decisions in cases involving alleged union unfair labor practices have affirmed that it is illegal for a union to:

a. Conduct mass picketing preventing employees or others from going into or leaving an employer's premises.

b. Commit acts of violence during a strike.

c. Threaten to injure non-striking employees.

d. Threaten employees that they will lose their jobs if they are not members in good standing of the union.

e. Not limiting the effect of its strike to the "primary" employer so as not to boycott neutral or secondary employers. There are exceptions to this in the garment and construction industries. In construction industries, for example, picketing is allowed on the job site if (1) picket signs make it clear that the dispute is only with the subcontractor; (2) picketing is limited to places and times the subcontractor's employees are present; (3) subcontractor's employees are doing normal subcontracting work at that site.

f. Picket or threaten to picket an employer to force him to bargain with a union not certified to bargain with that employer or (2) the striking union failed to win a majority of the employees' votes in an NLRB election within the last twelve months or (3) the picketing continues for more than thirty days without the union's filing a petition for election.

g. Enter into a "hot cargo" agreement with an employer whereby the employer agrees to stop doing business with another employer.

h. Fail (union or employer) to give sixty days' notice to federal and state conciliation services and opposing party of intent to change conditions of an existing contract.

Section 9 of the Taft-Hartley Act prescribes procedures for secret ballot, majority rule election of unions to represent employees and procedures by which the NLRB certifies that union as the exclusive bargaining agent for those employees.

Section 10 of the law directs the NLRB to investigate and adjudicate unfair labor practices and to petition appropriate US Circuit Courts for injunctive reliefs.

The law further provides that when, in the opinion of the President of the United States, a strike or lockout affects public safety, health, security, the President may ask the federal Circuit Court to direct that the action stop while the President appoints a board of inquiry to look into the dispute.

It further makes it unlawful for federal government employees to participate in a strike and directs that violators be discharged. Several years ago federal air transport controllers began a strike. The federal employees involved were fired and the union de-certified as the air traffic controllers' bargaining agent.

The Taft-Hartley law is very complex. Whether or not it has fulfilled its objectives of equalizing powers and restraints of labor and management and correcting perceived labor abuses, is a matter of opinion. In any event, further labor conflict encouraged the Congress to enact the Landrum-Griffin Act in 1959.

Landrum-Griffin Act

The Landrum-Griffin Act (Labor Management Reporting and Disclosure Act of 1959) resulted from concern for increasing corruption within organized labor.

In 1957 the Senate Select Committee on Improper Activities in the Labor or Management Fields investigated the extent to which criminal elements were engaged in labor-management activities.

Senator John L. McClellan's committee questioned minor hoods, tough racketeers, big time mobsters, reputable business leaders. Some witnesses hid behind the Fifth Amendment; others talked. Patterns emerged: labor racketeering, corruption, violence, roughshod treatment of union members. The Landrum-Griffin Act was meant to help labor clean up its act.

The Act provided a bill of rights for union members:

a. Equal rights and privileges for members to attend meetings, to debate, to vote.

b. Members' right to meet, to assemble freely, to express their views within the labor organization.

c. Restrictions on union dues, initiation fees, assessments; all to be determined by majority vote in secret ballot.

d. Members protected in their right to sue union or management and to witness before a court or labor board.

e. Safeguards against improper disciplinary action by the union.

f. Provisions of union constitutions not in accord with these basic rights would not be valid.

It also established the following:

a. The union must provide individual members with a copy of the bargaining agreement (contract), if they wish one, and must keep a file copy available for members' review.

b. The union must inform its members of the provisions of the Landrum-Griffin Act.

c. The union must provide detailed reports of its offices, constitution, officers, dues or fees, financial status, loans and other disbursements. Loans to union officers are limited to $2000 each.

d. Union funds cannot be used to pay the fine of anyone violating the Act.

e. Union officers must submit statements of personal financial worth for themselves and for their families.

f. Employers must report any payments, loans, gifts to the union or any management funds used to interfere with union activities.

g. Employers attempting to influence employees' organizing and bargaining collectively, or providing information about employee or union activities related to a labor dispute (other than that lawfully given before a court or government agency) must report their activity to the Secretary of Labor.

The Act attempted to reform union leadership by ruling that:

> "No person who is or has been a member of the Communist Party or who has been convicted of or served any part of a prison term . . . for robbery, bribery, extortion, embezzlement, grand larceny, burglary, arson, violation of narcotics laws, murder, rape, assault with intent to kill, assault which inflicts grievous bodily injury . . . or conspiracy to commit any of these . . . can serve as officer or consultant . . . for five years after the incident."

The Landrum-Griffin Act makes it unlawful for anyone to picket an employer for personal profit (other than improved wages, working conditions, etc.) by taking money or other things of value.

It also makes it unlawful for any person to restrain, coerce or intimidate any member of a labor organization in interference with any right entitled under the Landrum-Griffin Act.

It also makes it unlawful to threaten, coerce or restrain anyone to cause him to strike or to refuse to handle products of another employer; to cause him to deal with a union not certified as his employees' representative; to force him to give particular work assignments to employees of certain labor unions.

The Civil Rights Act of 1964

The Civil Rights Act of 1964 undertook to end all employment discrimination based on race, color, religion, sex or national origin in industries affecting interstate commerce. The law emphasizes conciliation in settling complaints of discrimination and provides for federal-state cooperation in enforcing its mandates. The Attorney General of the United States, without deferral to state or local agencies, can proceed directly against offendors where he finds a "pattern of resistance" to enjoyment of rights guaranteed by this and other civil rights laws.

I could not hope by this chapter to make the reader an expert on labor laws. I do hope, however, to make the reader more aware of the general intent of previous labor legislation and of the major provisions of these specific statutes. Any manager directly involved in a labor dispute should consult carefully and often with his company's legal staff.

As for the Security Director, the preceding chapters and this one should make him aware that in the past both labor and management have abused their powers and done things that were either illegal or unfair. All that leaves a bad taste in one's mouth long after the dispute at issue has been resolved. The Security Director and his staff must work closely with both disputants, before, during and after a labor crisis, as a referee to prevent violence and abuse of the law and to act as a calming influence. The more he knows of what has happened before and may happen again, what is proper and what is improper, how both parties reacted to these improprieties, the better he can keep the peace.

CHAPTER 4

LABOR RELATIONS AT THE GROUND LEVEL

The degree of success realized by any company largely depends on how well it handles its most difficult to manage asset—people. The productivity and efficiency of its people, at every level, are critical. And certain hard-to-measure, intangible ingredients—morale, personal dignity, sense of involvement—determine that productivity and efficiency. These ingredients are present in all who work, but only the skilled and thoughtful manager can make the most of them. I speak of labor relations.

Most companies like to think their management and employees are one big, happy family. Most think they provide good working conditions and ample rewards for work done—that there is no need for a union. If employees don't quite agree (and their concerns may be completely unjustified but they feel them anyway), and there seems to be a communications gap between employee and manager, enter a third party seeking to represent those employees in bargaining with that employer—the union.

Employees join unions and support union-directed labor disputes for a variety of reasons, such as:

a. A feeling that wages and benefits are not competitive with like jobs in like firms; are competitive but not adequate; are improperly administered.

b. A sense of insecurity in job tenure or advancement prospects, in communicating problems with management, in management's communicating matters of real importance (wages, benefits, other incentives) to them.

c. Unfair or inconsistent work standards.

d. Poor working conditions.

e. Poor or poorly spelled out personnel policies.

f. Inconsistencies or inequities in management's administration of policies, rules and regulations.

g. Management's simply not convincing employees that a third member of their family is not needed or desirable.

h. Group pressure and a need to belong. Often this is the key factor that keeps individuals on picket lines: "My buddy's here; I'm not going to let him down." In a prolonged dispute, group pressure and camaraderie become as critical (or more) than the original issues that sparked the picketing.[1]

To be successful, the union must promise and deliver remedies for these concerns: better wages, better working conditions, protection and equal treatment for the individual, a system for handling and resolving complaints against management, a voice in company policies.

Hopefully, the company's insistence on caring and professional management may make all that unnecessary. Employees will feel they don't need a union to speak for them. Too often, however, this is not the case.

When an employer learns that a union is attempting to organize his employees or is presenting a grievance he really believes unfair or that will totally disrupt his company (as in a strike), he often reacts in shock and dismay. No one likes to fail; no one likes to be misunderstood or treated unfairly. Not even the boss. He acts in haste.

If he shoots from the hip he is apt to make costly mistakes. Mistakes that may cause lengthy and costly litigation and may cause him to lose a fight he has no business losing.

For example, he may question employees improperly, threaten employees or the union, discharge or otherwise discipline employees for engaging in union activities. In each instance he is vulnerable to an unfair labor practices charge which could cost him the game. Or he might promise changes in wages, hours, working conditions that he really can't afford and are not wise.

He should not panic. He should get complete, accurate facts in the matter then calmly consider the choices of action open to him. He should get competent professional advice. This may come from his Personnel Director, his Director of Industrial Relations, his Security Director, his legal counsel, federal or state labor agencies.

Any action he takes should be completely and accurately documented. For example, if it is necessary to fire an employee, management should be able to answer:

a. Why was this action taken: What happened? Why is this individual responsible? Why not some other disciplinary measure?

b. Has the same action been taken against other employees for the same reason?

c. Were written or oral warnings and counselings given, if appropriate, for past incidents? Are they documented?

d. Was the worker known to be active in union affairs? Can his union activity reasonably be charged as grounds for this disciplinary action?

e. Is the worker's record fully and accurately documented: length of service; positions held; conduct; efficiency; work habits; wage increases; promotions; disciplinary actions; training; commendations?

f. Are there witnesses to critical conversations or other incidents affecting the employee?

The Security Director may be very much involved, particularly if the incident is related to Security Department activities. That's why he should know the procedures and responsibilities involved in the disciplining process.

He also should know that in a union's campaign to organize a company or to compete with other unions to be the NLRB-certified bargaining agent for that company's employees, the NLRB forbids unions to:

a. Coerce employees into joining the union.

b. Restrain or coerce an employer in selecting the union for collective bargaining.

c. Cause or attempt to cause an employer to discriminate against an employee by discouraging or encouraging membership in a particular union.

d. Causing or attempting to cause an employer to refuse to handle the product or refuse to do business with another employer.

e. Picketing for recognition of their union if the employer already has lawfully recognized another union as the collective bargaining agent.

f. Inducing or attempting to induce an employer to assign certain work to employees in a particular union or craft, or to try to maintain "union seniority" lists for preference in jobs, or to pay for services not performed.

g. Require employees under a union shop agreement to pay a union membership fee that is excessive or discriminatory.

Even when a union has become the NLRB-certified representative and a collective bargaining agreement signed into contract, the fight is not over. It has only begun. The contract must be administered; it must be enforced. Every day, every time, for the duration of the contract. The union will look after its rights in the agreement; management must do the same.

Management must assure that all managerial personnel, particularly supervisors who will have constant contact with the workers, thoroughly understand the contract. This should be done as soon as possible after it is signed and periodically during its term. The orientation should have four objectives:

a. Supervisors must clearly understand management's inherent and express rights and prerogatives and any limitations under the contract.

b. Supervisors must clearly understand the union's duties and responsibilities under the contract.

c. Supervisors must know how to answer employees' questions about the contract. If individual employees wish a copy, the union must provide it. The union also must maintain a copy for its members' review.

d. Supervisors must know how to deal with complaints, grievances, disciplinary matters; and how to handle, at their levels, the company's contractual obligations.

The role of the supervisors is critical. They are the ones who will administer the company's end of the contract, every day, in all circumstances and situations. If they do not understand the contract's language, it must be clarified. Supervisors must insist that neither company nor employee (union or non-union) rights be waived. Once waived or altered, it's hard to reclaim rights and their very definition may become "fuzzy."

Complaints or grievances should be handled at the lowest level possible with appropriate review by management's chain-of-command. That helps avoid error or allows an error to be remedied more quickly. It also keeps everything in perspective and assures that everyone concerned is properly informed.

When a formal grievance is filed, the company must promptly and thoroughly investigate it. If a grievance has merit, it should be resolved as quickly and as quietly as possible. On the other hand, management must consider the risk of establishing a precedent that may pinch its toes later on.

If the grievance has large fiscal or operational significance, or cannot be readily resolved by management and labor negotiators, it probably must go to arbitration. This is an informal trial in which management and labor submit evidence to an impartial arbitrator whose decision is binding on both parties.

Just as the arbitrator must be selected with great care, so must the individual who will represent the company's side of the argument.

Labor unions can provide individuals skilled at arbitration proceedings. The company would be foolish not to similarly protect its interests.

Sometimes the union decides to by-pass the contract's grievance procedures, to take direct action, such as a work slow down or a strike, to force its demands. Unless the complaint involves an unfair labor practice by management, this "end run" by the union may be illegal.

Sometimes the union uses the physical confrontation as a collective bargaining tactic to demonstrate power, to show member solidarity, or to put economic pressure on company negotiators. In these latter cases, the direct action may be legal — at least in the beginning.

"Direct action," legal or not, almost always means a very bad time for everyone concerned.

A strike is a war; a test of economic strength and of will, between the union and its members and supporters and the employer.

Excepting the true "wildcat strike," in which employees simply lay down their tools or walk off the job, often without informing the union beforehand, strikes don't just happen. The typical economic strike is calculated and deliberate. The union will have carefully considered its options and its resources. It certainly will have considered whether the strike can pressure the company to give up the union's demands. It will have considered likely company reaction to a strike and likely support of the strike by other unions, other employee organizations, the community.

Having decided on an economic strike, the union probably will prepare for it secretly until it is ready to confront management.

Most unions have constitutional procedures covering strikes, including members' vote on strike action and approval by the parent national union. In practice, however, union leadership pretty much controls the vote of its membership. If they choose to strike, they almost always can get the approval of their members.

Economic strikes need time to consider, to plan, to mobilize resources. They don't just happen; they are caused.

The most common causes of strikes are:

    a. To force recognition of a union.

    b. To pressure an employer during bargaining.

    c. To protest management's acts: discharges, layoffs, cutbacks, unfavorable handling of grievances.

    d. To show sympathy with another union or another local.

    e. To protest assignment of work to non-union employees or to employees of another union.

f. To force the employer to stop doing business with another employer.[2]

In labor disputes we hear the phrase, "We have a right to strike." That's another labor relations' phrase that is not too clear. It probably is meant to mean that no one can be made to work for someone else if he doesn't want to. One thing, however, *is* clear. There is no *unqualified* right to strike.

Strikes to support lawful labor objectives are constitutionally protected. The problem is to determine whether the particular objectives of a strike are "lawful." This hinges upon current federal and state labor laws and court decisions concerning them.

As a general rule, strikes are illegal when they are called for an unlawful purpose or are conducted in an unlawful manner. These are examples of strikes which may be unlawful:

a. "Sitdown" strikes where employees stop work and take possession of their employer's premises.

b. Strikes accompanied by violence. Even when begun as a "lawful" strike, they become "unlawful" when violence is *deliberately* injected.

c. Strikes in violation of federal law notice provisions: sixty days to the employer, thirty days to the Federal Mediation and Conciliation Service and to appropriate state labor agencies.

d. Strikes violating the provisions of federal law, as in defiance of existing union bargaining certifications; union jurisdictional strikes; strikes to require "hot cargo" contracts; certain secondary strikes or boycotts.

e. Strikes in violation of a valid no-strike clause in the current contract.[3]

The right to picket also is not an unqualified right. It depends upon the purpose of the picketing and how it is carried out. Peaceful picketing at the employer's premises is fine; mass picketing which denies entrance and exit from the facility is not.

The employer's rights greatly depend on the legality of the strike and its picketing. If the strike is *illegal*, picketing is unprotected by the authority of the NLRB and the employer has much greater latitude of action. If it is a *legal* strike, picketing is protected and the NLRB closely monitors and controls the employer's conduct. A valid economic strike, legal at the start, for example, may become illegal and unprotected by union picketing tactics. Similarly, an economic strike can become a protected unfair labor practice strike if the employer is guilty of an unfair labor practice during that strike.

An employer *cannot* fire employees for engaging in either an economic strike or in an unfair labor practices strike. He *can* hire replacements for striking employees, however, to keep his business operating.

Unfair labor practices strikers who give an unqualified offer to return to work must be accepted, even if that means terminating a "replacement."

Economic strikers do not have that absolute right to reinstatement upon termination of the strike. If the employer has hired a permanent replacement before the striker makes an unconditional offer to return to work, the employer is not required to fire the "replacement" and to accept the returning worker. He *is* obliged to give those returning workers first chance at other jobs that are available or come available.

The replacement of strikers is an extremely complex and technical subject. Employers should handle it only upon advice of their labor lawyer.

During a labor dispute, the employer should try to keep employees notified of the status of negotiations and may wish to publicize strike issues. He should go about this very carefully, however, as it involves sensitive legal questions. Improperly handled, it may trigger a valid unfair labor practices charge against the employer. The truth of the employer's communication with employees during a labor dispute is not as critical as to whether his purpose is to disparage or discredit the union in the eyes of the employees.

The NLRB allows an employer to communicate directly with employees so long as the communication is non-threatening and presents:

a. Information on the status of negotiations and the employer's last bargaining offer.

b. Explanations of positions previously advanced by the employer at the bargaining table or in a deposition of grievances.

c. Refutation of inflammatory charges openly made by the union.

d. Criticism of the union's bargaining strategy and certain related union leadership tactics which the company charges cause the dispute to remain unsettled.

The communications, however, must *not* be coupled with a *fixed* position by the employer at the bargaining table as this could be interpreted as an attempt to bypass and undermine the union by going direct to its membership.[4]

Employers' solicitation of striking employees to return to work also is a hazardous operation. Mere solicitation, so long as it is not accompanied by threats or promises, is lawful. But if the solicitation is proven to be part of a "pattern of legal opposition to the purpose of the law," or if it was conducted under circumstances and in a manner reasonably calculated to undermine the union, it becomes an unfair labor practice.

Employers usually limit their communications with striking employees to factual representations of the status of negotiations, the positions of both parties, assurances that the employees' jobs are available and the plant gates open for anyone wishing to return to work.

A union member who crosses a picket line to return to work may be fined by his union. The union may not fine a worker who is not a union member. If a union member effectively resigns from that union during a strike, then crosses the picket line to return to work, he cannot be fined by the union.

During the strike the employer has a right to protect his property and premises and to be assured free access to them. Local police are obligated to preserve public safety and order, to protect property and the civil rights of anyone affected in a labor dispute. Police actions may include prohibiting mass picketing, violence, coercion, intimidation, trespass, impeding ingress or egress to premises, fraud, misrepresentation. Employers usually must ask for and occasionally must demand this protection. Often they also must turn to courts for temporary restraining orders or injunctions.

Under the National Labor Relations Act, in certain circumstances an employer may lock his employees from the work place when an impasse in bargaining seems apparent. It is a highly risky operation from a legal standpoint, however, with many attendant problems: Has an impasse truly been reached? Can he hire replacements? Temporary or permanent? Does the employer have any other recourse? From a tactical standpoint, use of a lockout is risky for the employer and should be weighed very carefully before being used.

Strikes usually are settled when both parties have realistically evaluated their positions and determined that a compromise settlement can be lived with. Union compromises are more apt to come from pressure from employees who wish to return to work than from bargaining between negotiating committees.

When employees return to work, management—particularly line supervisors who work most closely with the majority of employees—should do everything possible to heal wounds opened during the strike. They must insist, however, that both parties meet all strike settlement agreements.

Running a successful business is a very complicated and difficult job. Labor relations are not the least of its demands. Although his responsibilities in labor relations essentially are limited to activities of his department, the Security Director must be aware of the overall industrial relations process and be particularly sensitive to labor-management problems in his own company. The better he does this the better he'll do his overall job of providing a safe and secure working environment for everyone involved.

CHAPTER 5

SECURITY STAFFS

There is a ballad, popular among British soldiers but whose sentiment has been adopted by soldiers of other armies. It speaks of the British soldier ("Tommy Atkins") who compared more than favorably with Alexander and Hercules while fighting, but was considered dirty and immoral when he was not. It goes like this:

> "While it's Tommy this, an' Tommy that, an' 'Tommy, fall be'ind,'
> But it's 'Please to walk in front, sir,' when there's trouble in the wind.
> There's trouble in the wind, my boys, there's trouble in the wind,
> O it's 'Please to walk in front, sir,' when there's trouble in the wind.

> "Then it's Tommy this, an' Tommy that, an' 'Tommy, 'ow's yer soul?'
> But it's 'Thin red line of 'eroes' when the drums begin to roll." — Rudyard Kipling

Sometimes security staffs may feel the sentiment applies a bit to them too. Sometimes they are reminded by some shortsighted managers that they produce no visible product, ostensibly contribute nothing to "the bottom line." And they can be costly, although in fact most operate on rather austere budgets. Unfortunately, if they do their work well, there is little of a tangible nature to prove it. Statistics, which may not be read, show a decline in criminal incidents or less damaged or lost company property. There may be an occasional executive memo or a pat on the back from the public relations department for some observed bit of professionalism by a security officer. These accolades, however, are easily overlooked.

All that is unfortunate, but it happens to other departments too and experienced Security Directors have learned to live with it.

Come a strike, however, and everyone will realize that those Security Officers are awfully nice to have around. If they have done their jobs well, even the more thoughtful striking employees may recognize their role as a peacekeeper and that, if Security Officers buffer management from their picket tactics, they also prevent unwanted clashes that could prolong lean times without paychecks.

At all times it is hard to imagine some part of the company which a good Security Director (or the executive who wears security as a second hat of responsibility) does not touch or should not touch. His job is to provide a safe and secure working environment for employees and visitors and to protect company property—buildings, equipment, money, products, information—from misuse, damage or loss. Considering the breadth of that assignment, one realizes that few days pass in which some member of the security staff does not touch, in some way, the people, equipment, facilities of every part of the corporate body. And that is a valuable resource to key company executives.

All managers should be constantly alert for signs of problems— mechanical or human—within their areas of responsibility. The sooner such problems are identified, the quicker they can be resolved so as not to interfere with company operations. Strike planning, to be discussed in the next chapter, usually begins with the earliest reported hints that a strike is possible. During negotiations, for example, managers' "testing the waters" must be a constant exercise, particularly as a contract's expiration date nears.

The security staff can help managers identify hot spots in labor-management relations. The Security Officer probably is the first company representative an employee sees on coming to work, the last to exchange greetings with him at the end of the day. If that Security Officer is well-groomed, professional in appearance and demeanor, reserved yet friendly to everyone, employees are going to return his greeting. And share confidences with him. Knowingly or unknowingly, they are going to reveal how their day has gone and, at times, what they intend to do about it when it has not gone well. I don't speak of spying; I speak of professional peacekeepers, keeping their fingers on the pulses of their patients, and alerting their supervisors to significant problems before those problems get out of hand.

Managers should recognize this asset and use it. They also should realize that they can help the security staff do security's job better. These managers, and their non-security staffs, also can be alert to security problems—something or someone that somehow just seems wrong. They should tell the Security Department about it. And those same managers can present a positive, official, supportive attitude toward security and urge their employees to do the same. Americans have a tendency to feel they have no personal stake in their local police department or in the activities of their company's police force on the job. They don't want to get involved. "Leave it to George. He's wearing a uniform and badge, not me." That's the common attitude. But a little suggestion and example by department heads, and a company-wide security education and awareness program, can go a long way to convince those employees that they really should be involved. After all, when a security problem exists it's their own lives and livelihood that are threatened.

Managers should take advantage of the security staff's familiarity with their departments and activities. And the idea that a Security Officer, making his rounds, may see things the manager might miss—the way a contractor goes about meeting safety or other contractual requirements on a company project—as, e.g., welders doing their thing with open flames too near paint or debris. Security staff and non-security managers can help each other and must be encouraged by company leadership to do so.

Those managers, however, should be willing to leave actual security-related decisions and management to the security professional. After all, it is *his* field. Let the production man handle production, the maintenance supervisor dispatch vehicles. Let the Security Director be the company's real security expert. That's what he's paid for—not the well-intentioned but sometimes painfully misinformed personnel man or purchasing director who argues security guard manning levels to provide "adequate guard coverage"; nor the plant engineer who constructs perimeter fencing. Let them do their things; let him do his.

The Security Director must be recognized as a key figure in company management. That can't be done by appointment alone; he must earn it. If he is not accepted as a key member of the management staff, he has a big sales job of his own and must realize that and go about it. Otherwise, he's not going to be able to do his job nearly as well.

He must be a free, equal, participating member of the overall manager staff. This is particularly true in strike planning and in strike operations. He must insist that it be so. Anything less only makes his job a lot harder and less likely to be done as well.

If the Security Director is experienced and highly motivated, he probably will do a good job. If he can add to those attributes outstanding physical, emotional and ethical fitness, he'll do even better. Even with limited resources he'll be able to hold up under a long haul; to handle crises with an even, calm temperament; to inspire confidence. Those things go a long way. And, because he probably will be imaginative too, he will have won the support and cooperation of other employees (strikers and non-strikers alike) and thus be able to do more with less "security resources."

He has a vital role in developing the company's strike management plan. He will be solely responsible for security aspects of that plan but, because his operations will touch those of all departments trying to operate in a crisis environment, he'll call attention to problem areas to be considered in all company activities. Shipping and receiving, for example, will have real problems in warehousing, in moving goods across picket lines, in protecting drivers. The Security Director can suggest security risks or additional topics they should consider and the means to minimize risks.

Once a strike begins, he will meet daily with other company crisis managers. Together they'll weigh the effectiveness of company operations to date, correct mistakes, modify procedures, attempt to forestall future problems.

He will be the company's primary liaison with local law enforcement and emergency agencies. Often he'll meet with other local or state officials or with representatives of federal agencies. All this is of vital interest to his company. And he must be constantly aware of the public relations' sensitivity of actions he and his staff take, particularly in dealing with activities on the picket lines.

He must be able to augment the company security staff with outside consultants or investigators, or to contract guards without seriously diluting the quality of protection. Often he'll have to meld these forces with his own on short notice. He must effectively blend these individuals into his own staff's operations. He'll also have to know how to secure and operate additional technical equipment (floodlights, cameras, tape recorders, night vision devices, etc.) to fulfill documentation requirements. All this means flexibility, imagination, cost awareness.

The Security Director must be personally responsible for orienting and supervising critical Observation and Documentation teams charged with noting and collecting evidence of any unfair labor practices or other illegal acts by striking employees or unions. The Security Director must see that this is done in a manner not likely to cause a violent confrontation yet so as to provide good legal evidence that can lead to injunctive relief if the company seeks it.

The security staff's reports and investigations of incidents of violence, damage, or loss of company or employee property or injury to individuals may lead to criminal charges by the company against responsible individuals. Certainly they may involve company expenditures of many thousands of dollars. Those reports and investigations must be executed well.

The security staff must be alert to modify strike control measures to lessen the chance of violence or to reduce its impact. This puts that security staff right in the trenches with striking employees. This is where maturity, discretion, common sense, emotional stability, professionalism count.

The Security Director and his staff are professional observers and keepers of the peace. They have no role at the bargaining table, no stake in the eventual terms of settlement of the dispute at hand. Their concern is to prevent or lessen violence while protecting people and property—no more and certainly no less. Whether this gives a temporary advantage to one side or the other is of no consequence. The security staff, particularly individual Security Officers and especially the security representative who will deal with picket captains or other leaders, must show no partiality, no bias and no opinions in the dispute.

They should not talk with striking employees, unless directed to do so, and should politely refuse any favors or gratuities. It's simple, either you're compromised or you're not. Violence erupts when a smirk, a gesture (particularly one perceived as obscene), a flippant remark is directed toward an individual who is himself frightened, unsure, excited, in an unfamiliar and stressful situation at a time when he feels his livelihood and family threatened.

Sooner or later the labor dispute will be resolved. When it is, workers will return to their jobs. If the security staff has remained neutral, professional, mature throughout the strike, workers at the main gate will find their first morning's glimpse of a friendly Security Officer reassuring and encouraging. That will go a long way toward healing bitterness engenderered during a strike.

The role of the security staff during a labor crisis is not an easy one. No one has an easy time during a strike, but the security staff's role is particularly difficult and unusually sensitive. That responsibility can best be met if the Security Director is competent, highly motivated, professional in all respects; if the security staff is well-trained and disciplined; if both have earned the respect and support of the majority of the employees.

If the Security Director has *not* done his homework beforehand by carefully selecting, training, disciplining, organizing his security force; by preparing and assuring understanding of standing operating procedures and techniques; by training individuals to be able to apply basic concepts and techniques in new and unexpected situations, he may be in for a very hard time during a strike. And chances are he's not going to have much time between a strike alert and the strike itself to make up for lost or neglected time in any of these areas.

If he *has* done his homework, however, and if it includes having on hand a basic strike management plan, particularly security aspects of that overall plan, he'll go into that strike with confidence that he can accomplish his mission with minimum risk to human relations and minimum economic costs.

While his assistants prepare the Security Department for strike duty, the Security Director sits with other company managers to develop the company's overall strike strategy. We turn now to pre-strike planning.

CHAPTER 6

PRE-STRIKE OPERATIONS

The Constitution of the United States guarantees workers' right to refuse to work under conditions they believe to be unfair. It also gives the employer the right to protect his investment and to defend his policies and work standards. When these rights clash, results can be bitter and violent.

Responsibility for preserving public order during these disputes is shared by labor, management, the security staff and local police. This means more than a tip of the hat by labor and management to legal requirements. It means an honest effort by both sides to resolve differences without violence or other illegal acts and to cooperate with the security staff and public agencies attempting to maintain order.

Not all labor battles feature violence, but it's likely whenever bitterness exists between many employees and the struck employer, when violence is deliberately used (or encouraged) by one side or the other, or when an incident or misunderstanding triggers it. The last—a garbled announcement, an insulting remark or gesture, the presence of an executive symbolic in the dispute—can be the hardest to anticipate. And it can be the most violent because it involves real anger.

Maintaining order in a strike begins with the earliest recognition that one is possible. It may be an economic strike, as discussed earlier, or it may be an unfair labor practice strike. In either case, the Security Director should know beforehand that a strike is possible or likely.

A good Security Director can't wait until picket lines close his gates or his facility becomes beseiged. No matter how much or how little warning he may get, he should be ready to take the first steps to restore order in the dispute.

He already should have on hand a basic Security Strike Plan, directing specific responsibilities and actions to preserve or restore order. This emergency plan should have been prepared in cooperation with other company managers and approved by the company's leadership. It can't

54

cover all situations, but at least it should start management moving in the right direction.

If such a plan does not exist, or to make one current, company managers must meet as early as possible to exchange information, to coordinate planning and activities, to assign responsibilities.

Creating defenses always is easier when one knows tactics he may have to face. Union tactics may be to disrupt company operations by:

a. Picketing premises.

b. Preventing or discouraging movement of raw materials or finished products into or out of the struck facility.

c. Intimidating employees crossing picket lines by embarrassment, harrassment, violence.

d. Slowing down company operations by any other means possible.

Management, on the other hand, will try to continue operations by:

a. Encouraging employees to come back to work.

b. Replacing striking employees.

c. Maintaining at least partial operations.

d. Maintaining free entrance and exit for personnel, raw material, finished products.

e. Attempting, by legal restraints or by agreements with the union, to limit the extent and manner of picketing.

The better the Security Director understands the disputants' goals and tactics, the better his chance of reasoning among them and avoiding confrontations. His own tactics begin with planning and other pre-strike preparations.

Even though the security staff may have written orders covering routine daily activities (prescribed guard rounds, protection devices, reports, communication systems, etc.), strike operations call for specific and unusual procedures.

A strike changes the whole situation. There probably will be more guards, different guard posts or clock rounds, special teams for observation and documentation. The facility itself will change. Certain gates will be closed; others will require more than usual protection. Some buildings may be shuttered with others activated. The Security Director must weave additional resources into his basic protection plan. Non-security managers and staffs become more involved with the Security Department. Hazards to personnel and property become much more real.

Planning reduces the risk of hasty or ill-conceived decisions, thus lessening chances of confrontations. The planning process necessarily requires early coordination and information sharing with other managers and staffs, vital during a labor dispute.

Those conferences should produce management decisions necessary to firm security plans. They might include the following items:

a. Will the company attempt to conduct "business as usual"?

b. How will access to the facility be handled?

c. What will be the probable size of the work force on the first day of the strike?

d. Will some workers and managers remain inside the struck facility during the strike?

e. Will alternate means of transportation or car pooling be required for managers and workers to cross picket lines?

f. Will shipments be made and received during the strike?

g. Where will the emergency staff work? Where will the rest of the regular management staff be established?

h. What will be the emergency chain-of-command and what special assignments given emergency team members?

i. Will construction projects or other contract work continue during the strike?

m. When police make arrests, will criminal complaints follow?

n. What documentary coverage of the strike will be necessary?

o. Is the company considering a lockout?

p. What pre-strike concessions may be granted strikers?

q. What company benefits are likely for striking employees? How will they be handled (will they require access to the facility)?

r. Will the company be responsible for strike-related damages to employees' property?

The Security Director won't make these basic decisions. They are not his responsibility. But he should be prepared to discuss security considerations in each of them. Once these decisions are made, however, security aspects of carrying them out will be his responsibility.

The company may believe it symbolically important that company operations continue during the strike—to show customers, the business world, the community and its employees that it will not be buffaloed; that the strike is ineffective. This goal may have nothing to do with economic considerations. It simply is showing the flag, waving it in the face of the strikers.

Sometimes that can be a very dangerous tactic. Sentiments run high in a strike. Continuing to operate can cause a violent reaction, especially when most employees are behind the union or when it's doubtful whether the company can operate during a strike. If the tactic fails, it can prolong the strike. Trying to conduct "business as usual" also could alienate the community or irritate a local police department, straining to meet all its public safety requirements on a very limited budget. On the other hand, if the company can do it, it weakens union strength, discourages strikers, encourages management.

Whether to operate or not operate often depends on the nature of the business. Some businesses (public utilities, health care facilities) have no choice. They have to operate. Other considerations might be customer demands, the resolve of striking employees, the availability of some workers to keep production and distribution going, the company's ability to obtain supplies.

The goals and overall strategy of management also can influence whether a company will try to operate during a strike. It may wish to crush the union and sees this as the way to do it. It may feel that it can operate the facility with the management staff alone. If it works, management gains a big psychological advantage which can shorten the strike.

Some managers feel it best to time any operations restrictions. Some say that if they can show from the start that they can conduct "business as usual," they'll reassure customers and discourage strikers. Others believe that if, at the start of the strike, they announce that the plant may go out of business or cannot hope to return to normal operations in the foreseeable future, they'll give striking employees a lot to think about. Some managers try for a combination of approaches: initially restricting plant operations then, as the strike progresses, resuming normal or near-normal operations to demonstrate that the strike just is not working.

To operate or not to operate is one of the toughest decisions in a labor dispute. The Security Director won't make it. That's not his job. But he'll have security-related input on it and, once the decision is made, he'll have a big part of the responsibility for carrying it out.

A second tough decision involves shipping and receiving. The strikers will attempt to prevent or discourage persons from entering the struck facility and the movement of raw material in or out. The law prohibits barring entrance and exits but pickets usually will attempt it anyway until police enforce that law. Usually it takes a legal complaint from the company before police do so. The company must anticipate strikers' tactics and ways to prevent or minimize the effect of those tactics.

Another decision involves use of gates to the struck facility. Restricting the number of gates reduces likely flashpoints. Two or three gates can be protected far easier than five or six. And activities at those fewer gates can be easier documented for possible legal action. Management must choose the best gates for its purposes and close the rest.

In pre-strike planning, management also must consider traffic and parking inside the facility during the strike. The idea is to provide the fastest and most direct routes between selected gates and work areas.

Planners also must consider using special identification badges during the strike and the control of visitors. Again, not the Security Director's decision alone, but he'll have to make it work.

Management's version of the strike is the lockout. It refuses to allow union members to work. It's a lawful tactic in some instances but, as discussed earlier, it runs a strong risk of being labeled an unfair labor practice. The lockout is a tactic management must consider carefully and early in prestrike planning.

Managers also must estimate the number of non-striking employees who will return to work and the problems they'll face crossing picket lines. This estimate affects logistics planning (*e.g.*, provision of company transportation, on-site meals and lodging, security planning for protective measures).

A very important pre-strike decision involves naming supervisors and managers and key workers who will remain inside the facility at all times during the strike. Most of the security staff, for example, will be there. They can't respond to an emergency if they can't get through picket lines. Other members of the emergency staff (engineers, electricians, etc.) may have to remain inside too. Once that decision is made, planners must address the big logistics and morale problems it generates. And the Security Director must add protection of these key personnel to his own list of responsibilities.

Use and control of access gates also is critical. Management must plan to consolidate shipments so they'll cross picket lines as little as possible and when local police (outside the perimeter) and the company security staff (inside the perimeter) can best observe and protect them.

Other decisions in shipping and receiving may include selection of outside warehousing and additional storage requirements on the struck facility; trucking between outside warehousing and the facility; necessary security protection for it all.

Very early the company must designate an emergency chain-of-command for the strike. Someone must have overall authority and responsibility to make final decisions for the company. During a strike the emergency chain-of-command may run directly from the senior executive present to the Security Director, although normally there might be one or more intermediary managers involved.

Pre-strike decisions also would include the location (usually off-site) of the rest of the management staff. That location and the extent of planned operations may dictate more security considerations for the Security Director.

Companies usually set up two emergency operations centers in the struck facility. One, a General Operations Center, is responsible for general operations and overall company strike strategy. The other, a Security Operations Center, is responsible for all security operations during the strike. The two groups should have "open-line" communications with each other and be physically close to expedite coordination. The senior company executive present should be with the General Operations Group; the Security Director with the Security Operations Group. More will be discussed later on both groups and both headquarters.

If construction projects are underway or planned for the near future, management must decide whether they will continue during the strike. It also must decide whether certain continuing maintenance operations will require striking union technical specialists' entering the facility during the strike. These projected activities must be included in the Security Director's security operations plans.

The legal staff must meet with other management representatives to determine the company's criminal complaint policy, documentary coverage of the strike, handling of company benefits during the strike, any pre-strike concessions to the union.

Local police are required to cooperate with management and union leaders in maintaining order, protecting people and property, assuring civil rights. They are limited, however, by physical resources available to them and by political constraints. They just can't respond as quickly, as firmly, and as cooperatively as management would like. They'd rather not make arrests in strike situations unless absolutely necessary. Arrests are an administrative bother to them when their attention may be needed in more critical areas. And making arrests usually does not win votes, particularly when those arrested are the voters. Arrests, when used with restraint and common sense, help prevent strike violence; unnecessary arrests, however, provoke ill will and may trigger that same violence.

When police arrest an individual, there is a presumption among most citizens that that arrest probably was justified. If prosecution does not follow, as when there is an agreement between company and union (normally as an amnesty clause to the strike settlement) that the company will not press charges for strike-related offenses, the police are caught in the middle and made to look foolish. They don't care for either situation.

Blanket amnesties make illegal, dangerous acts permissable collective bargaining tools. This is not in anyone's best interest. The Security Director should make that point.

He must live, however, with whatever decision management makes on the question of strike-related arrests. It helps to have that decision early in the game. Will trespassers, vandals, saboteurs—those who physically threaten or actually harm employees or employees' property, or company property—actually be prosecuted for those offenses? The Security Director has a right to know. If they say they will prosecute, managers should stick to their guns. And the Security Director must inform strikers and local police of that intent, as early as possible, so that everyone dances to the same tune.

Legal counsel also must suggest the type and amount of documentary coverage (movies, photos, sound, witness' statements) required for the injunctive relief which almost certainly will be needed soon after the strike begins. Once that decision is made, the Security Director will have to provide that documentary evidence. So he must plan how to get it.

The legal and personnel staffs also must decide what company benefits (pay, health insurance, unemployment compensation, etc.) should be allowed striking employees and how they will be handled. Administering those benefits will involve planning and coordination by the Security Director to assure coverage of benefit distribution points or other areas which might involve confrontations between management and strikers.

Management also must determine company policy on compensating non-striking employees for personal injuries suffered passing through picket lines or for damage to their automobiles or other personal property (including their private residences) in a bitterly contested strike. The Security Director will have to investigate these incidents, determine responsibility, and gather evidence for possible use in civil or criminal court. He must plan ahead now, before the picket lines close, on equipment and personnel he'll need to get that job done.

Any pre-strike concessions to be granted the union or individual employees also should be determined now. Pre-strike concessions set dangerous precedents and should be avoided. The union will seek them under the guise of "keeping the strike peaceful." For example, they may ask the following:

a. Agreements allowing workers to return, at their convenience, to pick up tools or work shoes or otherwise "clean out their lockers."

b. Agreements restricting production activity during a strike and allowing union representatives periodically to "inspect" for compliance.

c. Agreements by which the company agrees to notify the union, in advance and as a "courtesy," of truck arrivals and departures.

d. Agreements by which the company agrees to certain allowable "trespass" by pickets.[5]

Management should be wary of any pre-strike concessions to striking employees. Once given, they can't be reclaimed. They cause problems as they occur and may set the stage for later "breach of faith" claims by the union. They are attempts at seizing and controlling company property during the strike and may even give the impression of "strike by mutual consent."

Once a strike begins, any concessions must be considered on a case by case basis and, if approved, closely monitored by the Security Director. This will be at times when there is the least amount of other activity and when he can give it close attention.

During pre-strike coordination and planning meetings, the legal staff must advise other managers on:

a. The type strike anticipated and its legal ramifications for both sides.

b. Noteworthy previous strike occurrences at that facility or others by the union presently involved.

c. Legal redress appropriate to the particular situation and how it can be obtained.

d. Whether an attempt should be made to replace striking workers and the legal and practical ramifications of that decision.

e. Limits to the authority and responsibility of the emergency staff to be operating within the facility.

f. Responsibilities of the company's *lone* press representative during the strike: What will be his authority? What restraints will be placed on him? What provisions are made for legal review of material released to the public?

g. Federal, state, municipal ordinances affecting company strike operations. For example, requirements for wording on strike gate signs.

h. Wording (and legal staff's review) of all company communications with employees to assure that the company is not vulnerable to an unfair labor practices charge.

i. Legal staff's role in supervisors' orientations.

j. Legal staff's determination whether the union has met the required sixty days' notice to the company of its intent to change the existing contract and the required thirty days' notice to the Federal Mediation and Conciliation Service and to appropriate state agencies. The legal staff probably will not query agencies about the thirty days' notice until just before the contract expires as any strike short of thirty days' notice would be illegal. That would force postponement of the strike.

k. Necessary coordination between the legal staff and management (particularly with the Security Director) in testing picket lines and documenting picketers' illegal acts or other unfair labor practices.

l. Assuring immediate availability of legal counsel, particularly to the Security Director, during the strike.

The company's legal staff should work with the Security Director in notifying municipal, county and state law enforcement agencies (verbally and in writing) of the pending strike. That report might contain the following information:

a. The company's name, business address, telephone number.

b. The international and local unions' names, addresses, telephone numbers.

c. Employer's kind of business.

d. Number and occupations of employees involved in the dispute.

e. Date the strike was (may be) declared.

f. Date strike became (to become) effective.

g. Anticipated number and occupation of employees expected to continue working during the strike.

h. Anticipated number of pickets.

i. Trouble anticipated.

j. Kind of strike (sympathy, wildcat, lockout, secondary, economic).

k. Any pre-strike concessions or agreements.

l. Preliminary planning *re* shift changes, operations' restrictions, gate designations, shipping/receiving, employees remaining on site, or other details that will help police determine the amount and type police involvement anticipated.

When the strike begins, the company must follow this preliminary report with one that is more detailed and accurate. It should cite exact limits of company property; gates designated for particular purposes; locations most likely to see conflict, trespass or questions of jurisdiction.

Similar, but not necessarily as detailed, reports of the impending or actual strike should be furnished any special police (as for rail or water shipments); fire departments or other emergency agencies; state and federal labor agencies.

It is very important that now and during the strike a record be kept of all communication with law enforcement agencies and with the union or other employee groups and their responses. This record must contain as much detail as possible:

a. When made, by whom, respondent.

b. What was said.

c. What was done as a result of that communication.

The General Operations Center should maintain logs for this purpose but, early in the planning phase, the Security Director should remind management of the need for such documentation, then periodically spot check to see that it is being done and being done properly.

Pre-strike coordination and planning meetings also must result in specific individuals being designated to handle specific strike-emergency responsibilities, such as the following:

a. Assignments to the emergency staff and establishment of the emergency chain-of-command.

b. Assignments to the General Operations Center and to the Security Operations Center.

c. Any augmentation to the Security Operations Group by other management personnel.

d. Assignments for plant supervisors to assume responsibility in the following areas:

(1) Personnel.

(2) Security (if not already designated).

(3) Operations/manufacturing.

(4) Legal.

(5) Public relations.

(6) Purchasing/Contracting.

(7) Distribution.

(8) Transportation.

(9) Maintenance (plant/vehicle/equipment).

(10) Engineering

e. Assignments to prepare or modify existing General Operations Plans with annexes.

f. Delegation to the Security Director of authority and responsibility to conduct a security survey of the facility and directing all other managers to assist as requested, particularly to take immediate corrective action on discrepancies noted in their departments.

Planning groups will meet informally, as required, to formulate the overall General Strike Plan and to resolve problems developing in the labor dispute.

When all annexes of the General Strike Plan have been reviewed and updated, management will approve the overall plan and, if appropriate, put it into effect.

The plan will be shown, in its entirety, only to necessary management leaders (those who are both authorized to know and have a valid need to know its details). The General Strike Plan is discussed in detail in a later chapter.

If time does not permit this detailed planning and coordination, the company must go with what it has, hopefully not making too many mistakes as the strike intensifies.

The Security Director must provide strong, competent, continuing leadership during the emergency, not only within his own department but in all management functions. If he is prepared, he'll be able to preserve order or at least greatly reduce disorder.

Even if he already has some form of Security Strike Plan on paper, he'll need to gather current information and rethink his strategy in view of the current situation.

He also must use this critical time before the strike to meet with strike leaders, possibly in cooperation with local police, to establish ground rules for picketing and other union activities during the strike.

Such meetings are to guarantee public order. That should be established at the start — not issues in dispute between labor and management; nor the overall strategy of either side — only preserving order, protecting property, insuring civil rights.

If all parties know exactly what will be allowed at plant gates or on the nearby streets, there is little chance of misunderstandings that can lead to trouble. The following ground rules, for both sides, might be established:

a. Force or violence will not be tolerated.

b. The law will be enforced with strict impartiality.

c. The rights of the public using the streets and sidewalks will be protected.

d. Unlawful conditions or acts which lead to disorder will not be tolerated.

e. The employment of professional bullies and thugs will not be tolerated.

f. Activities of professional agitators will not be tolerated.

g. Use of language or manner of address, or other acts which are offensive to public decency, or which may provoke violence, will not be tolerated.

h. The right of striking employees to conduct orderly picketing will be fully protected.

i. The number of pickets and their manner of picketing shall be agreed to by both parties and will be enforced. Pickets may peacefully encourage others not to enter the struck facility or to leave it but, if those individuals choose to enter or leave, that right will not be denied them.

j. Striking employees may picket in the vicinity or in front of the place of employment to:

(1) Persuade those still employed to strike.

(2) Persuade those considering employment with the company not to do so.

(3) Inform customers and the general public about the strike.

It also should be understood that respective labor and management leaders will be accountable for their own groups and for enforcing this agreement.

Most important, the Security Director must try to establish mutual trust among all the leaders concerned. The one thing that most surely determines whether violence will be a part of a labor dispute is distrust. Management does not trust labor; labor does not trust management; neither trusts the police and, perhaps to a degree, company security.

It also will greatly help the situation if the parties concerned can agree at this time to maintain close relations during the disturbance. Each party (union/management/security staff/local police) should designate individuals who will be responsible for keeping the others informed and for receiving communications for their groups. For the employer, this should be the Security Director. For the union, it almost always will be the strike committee chairman or the chief picket captain.

Proper prior planning, coordination, information sharing and a cooperative spirit, all strongly supported and exemplified by the Security Director, can go a long way to resolving a labor dispute without violence.

Let's now consider the steps the Security Director must take in gathering information, in evaluating security risks and in planning protective measures.

CHAPTER 7

RISK ANALYSIS

The first step to improving a company's security is to assess its present vulnerabilities, measures being taken to reduce those vulnerabilities, likely threats to those vulnerable areas.

A security survey points out and weighs safety and security hazards to which the company (facility) may be vulnerable at any time. In a potential strike situation, pre-strike intelligence collection and analysis in terms of that security survey may indicate immediate risks occasioned by the strike threat.

The Security Director can use both assessments to devise measures to reduce those risks.

Conduct of a thorough security survey and collection and analysis of information for intelligence data about a potential strike are valuable pre-strike operations important to the Security Director.

The security survey should identify critical areas or functions within the company. Those whose partial or complete loss would have an immediate, serious, long-range impact on the ability of that company to survive and to operate as intended.

It also should identify the company's vulnerabilities: areas or functions susceptible to sabotage, work stoppages, industrial espionage, fire, explosions or other major disasters.

It then should identify the hazards most likely to affect that vulnerability. They might be man-made: intentional acts of commission or omission, or human weaknesses which unintentionally cause damage, loss or compromise. They might be natural hazards: storms (cyclone, tornado, hail, etc.); earthquakes; floods (also possible by human action); fire (also possible by human action); temperature extremes.

The study must weigh all these factors, critically consider protective measures, then recommend well thought out, viable changes or additions that would lessen the company's security risk.

If the Security Director has been on-site for some time, he already should have completed an informal security survey of his facility. At the very least he should be mentally aware of likely problem areas. That's a start. If a strike is in the offing, however, he must quickly review those known problem areas and search out any more.

Security surveys should not be conducted as clandestine affairs, nor in a vacuum. They should be done openly, in a professional manner, welcoming input by everyone concerned. The Security Director may not agree with the type or degree of risk reported through the survey, nor with the recommendations for correcting it, but he can't go wrong by listening and appreciating the effort and interest of the individual making the report.

The survey should be as complete and detailed as time and resources permit. It should include all physical facilities and all company operations. It should cover all shifts, day and night, weekends and holidays, as well as work days. It should cover areas outside a facility's perimeter as well as everything inside it.

It would include many topics. Such as the following:

a. General information on the facility itself: location, size, building and area use, sensitive areas and sensitive operations, stock piles, construction.

b. Information on staff and employee functions, number of employees, union involvement, shift schedules, gate use, inventory procedures, maintenance, vendor services, products.

c. Identification of critical areas and equipment.

d. Identification of vulnerabilities.

e. Physical security requirements, such as the following:

(1) Perimeter fencing.

(2) Perimeter gates and doors.

(3) Critical interior gates and doors.

(4) Lighting.

(5) Power and emergency power systems.

(6) Locks and padlocks.

(7) Key control.

(8) Buffer zones.

(9) Signage; marking of company property.

(10) Alarm systems.

(11) Closed circuit television (CCTV) protection.

(12) Fire alarm and fire fighting equipment/systems.

(13) Access controls.

(14) Shipping and receiving.

(15) Purchasing and contracting.

(16) Property control.

(17) Vehicle maintenance.

(18) Plant and equipment maintenance.

(19) Computer security.

(20) Security of cash and other valuables.

(21) Housekeeping services; garbage, trash, salvage.

(22) Mail and parcel post facilities.

(23) Dining facilities.

(24) Vending services.

(25) Communications.

f. Security of proprietary information.

g. Personnel security.

h. Safety.

i. Medical support.

j. Security and safety training and awareness.

k. Liaison with local police and with other agencies.

l. Record of theft, vandalism, sabotage, misuse of company property.

m. Emergency planning:

(1) Planned steps to minimize the physical effects of man-made or natural disasters.   ·

(2) Planned steps after an emergency to replace key individuals permanently or temporarily unable to perform their normal roles.

(3) Planned steps after an emergency to restore production or other facility operations.

More specific information on the actual conduct of security surveys is contained in the following chapter.

The Security Director must analyze security survey reports prepared by his staff and, applying his experience and judgment, prepare a written summary with specific recommendations to correct discrepancies.

Management must treat that report as a sensitive, classified document to be discussed only with those persons authorized to have the information it contains and a clear need for it.

Because of economic or time restrictions only a few corrective actions may be possible. Even then considerable time probably will elapse before permanent systems to correct discrepancies can be operational. During the interim, the Security Director must use imagination (signage, decoy cameras, lighting, adjustment of guard rounds or fixed posts, other measures) to improvise temporary security measures.

Company managers must be directed to correct noted security or safety weaknesses within their own areas of responsibility. They should be given a time limit to effect those corrections. When that time has passed, the Security Director should follow-up to insure that corrective action has been taken.

Even though discrepancies can't be immediately corrected, the Security Director's awareness of their existence is a form of showing the security flag. He has been alerted to potential risks and, to anyone who might wish the company harm, presumably will plan to do something about those known risks. This is a particularly valid exercise in pre-strike operations. If an employee is considering means to interrupt company operations and realizes that security is being tightened, he is going to have second thoughts about risking that interruption.

Security staff activities in conducting security surveys also will show that they care about employees' security and safety and about protecting company property. That goes a long way.

As he tasks selected members of his staff to survey the company's safety and security posture, the Security Director will ask others to provide additional information he'll need for his Security Strike Plan.

He'll want to know about the current union contract. When does it expire? What is the anticipated strike date? Are there particular clauses in the contract (no strike, no lockout) that might affect the strike? Has the union given the prescribed strike warning notices?

He also will want to know more about the union itself. Where is it located? Who are its leaders (national/local)? How large is its membership? What are its affiliations with the national union? How are other unions likely to support the striking local? What has been the past record of both the national and local unions for strike activities? Have they been characterized by violence? Have union leadership kept their word on any other agreements with the company or with the Security Department? How have union leaders regarded the security staff in the past?

The Security Director also will want to know the attitudes of local officials and the news media toward the company, the union, the strike threat.

How has the community responded to any previous strikes at the company? How might they feel about current issues in dispute? How dependent on the company is the local economy? What are the chances of sympathy strikes or other displays of solidarity between other unions in the area and the striking local?

How effective are local law enforcement agencies? In the past, how enthusiastic have they been in controlling disorder and violence during a strike? What might be their reaction this time?

The Security Director also will want to know of any expressions of intent by the striking unions or other local unions. Has anything appeared on local television or in local newspapers? Has the union printed pamphlets or other material that might indicate tactics they'll use to enforce their demands?

As staff members research public and company documents for this information, all should be alert to more immediate and current signs. In the plant and in the community they'll hear things about the strike and the direction it probably will take. Much of that information may translate into valuable intelligence for the Security Director.

It can come from a variety of sources. For example, the best source may be from the union itself. Knowingly or unknowingly, individual workers will drop hints to their supervisors or others. Hints confirming an impending strike action; hints concerning union demands; hints concerning union tactics to win those demands.

Staff members may note a change in employees' attitudes. Sulleness or open hostility toward supervisors. It may be reflected in a sudden rash of complaints or grievances, often flippant in nature or of little real substance but brought forward as complaints anyway.

Negotiators report changes in union posture at the bargaining table or hints of interference or other action by the national union. All of it may indicate impending action.

Other clues to a possible strike or its direction or length might be the presence or absence of seasonal work to tempt employees to strike when normally they might not. For example, in a farming community workers might prefer simply to stay at home and mind their farms for awhile than to work at the struck company. If other outside employment is available, loss of the company's pay check isn't so critical and workers may be more tempted to strike.

If local merchants and banks, or the company credit union, report sudden interest in new loans or in credit extensions, it could be another indication that an industrial storm is brewing.

The availability of union strike benefits could indicate the same thing. Workers are more apt to strike if they know they have some economic help to fall back on.

And there will be open pre-strike activities by the union—such things as unexpected and more frequent meetings of the union leadership, particularly strike committee activity; the union's leasing local space for a strike headquarters or procuring certain equipment such as radios, sound trucks, office equipment. Preparation of picket signs is a strike indication, as would be the appearance of notices, handbills or pamphlets in which the union openly states its intent to strike.

Espionage directed toward the striking union or its members is illegal. Management staffs can be alert, however, for bits of information as cited above. When sifted and carefully evaluated, they may form intelligence that can be of great help to the Security Director.

Awareness of his own weaknesses, as revealed by the security survey of his company, and of possible action by the union and its members to exploit those weaknesses, is very important as the Security Director considers his own strategy to insure his company's security.

CHAPTER 8

SECURITY SURVEYS

In surveying his facility to determine safety and security risks and appropriate protective measures, the Security Director should use the help of carefully selected security staff members.

He might conduct the survey himself. Certainly there are aspects of it, such as certain highly sensitive company operations, that he may have to do himself. He has the most expertise in the security field. But security surveys take time, a lot of time. He has other responsibilities that, in a pre-strike situation, can't wait. Besides, working alone, he may miss things. Two heads, or more, usually are better than one, if only to notice more things and report them. The Security Director, working in a quiet and uninterrupted atmosphere, can interpret and evaluate individual security survey team reports, following up on them as necessary.

Members of the security staff probably will know more about day-by-day operations of the facility, at the grass roots' level where problems are most likely to occur, than would that Security Director. They are more apt to recognize the same sensitive areas and functions a striking employee would know.

And participating in a facility's security survey is an excellent training device for key security staff members. It teaches them and it motivates them. They will experience more of a personal role in protecting employees and property and undoubtedly will welcome the chance to express their own opinions in security planning.

For his survey team, the Security Director should select the most experienced, most mature, most capable individuals. Those individuals also would be recognized for their ability to get along well with other employees and supervisors. No one knows a particular department or physical area within a plant better than the people who work in that department or area every day. They know the critical elements of that area or operation and hazards to them. Perhaps they can't suggest the best protection against those hazards, but they probably will have some ideas worth considering. Again, the bonus is that involving employees gives them a sense of belonging and an awareness that the company cares about them and the work they do.

The Security Director should personally brief and debrief survey team members. The debriefing should include his going over each report with the individual who prepared it. That way he'll be sure he understands exactly what the observer noted and can send that individual for further information if necessary. The observer will profit by that debriefing and feel that his work is appreciated. The Security Director should be particularly demanding in accepting initial reports. Let him set high standards and insist that his staff meet them.

Before they begin their work, survey team members should read and be sure they understand any previous surveys. In a pre-strike survey, surveyors must keep in mind physical and functional changes the strike may cause: restricted gate use; revised use of large areas and buildings; changes in traffic and parking patterns; additional security systems (lighting, alarms, CCTV, etc.).

The security survey must include all critical facility operations and areas, areas immediately beyond the facility's perimeter, day and night operations, all shifts, both work and non-work days.

All individuals conducting security surveys should be equipped with detailed checklists, provided by the Security Director, to focus their thinking on areas his experience indicates should be covered and suggesting minimum requirements for adequate safety and security coverage. The checklists, however, cannot be all inclusive and must have extra blank spaces to encourage the individual surveyor to exploit his own initiative and thinking.

The remainder of this chapter suggests areas and operations which should be examined as part of the security survey of a facility. It too is not all inclusive. The Security Director should consider them in terms of his own requirements then prepare checklists relevant to his own facility.

A good place to start an audit of any firm's physical security is at the perimeter of the company's property.

Perimeter Security

a. Signage.

Signage (property limits, restrictions, gate use, directions, traffic control, etc.) must be adequate (number, size, wording), appropriate, properly placed, clearly visible, in good repair. Signs should be current, that is support the overall strike management plan, by reflecting any strike-occasioned changes to the facility or its operations.

b. Buffer Zones.

(1) Cleared zones, free of debris or other material or growth that would provide concealment or hinder observation by the security staff or local police, must be established and maintained fifteen to twenty yards (if possible) on both sides of the perimeter barrier.

(2) The security surveyor should carefully check paths or roads coming close to the perimeter and be alert for makeshift ladders or other means of crossing the fence. They indicate activity focusing on a particular part of the perimeter.

(3) Security patrols must periodically check buffer zones for signs of intrusion; damage to perimeter barriers, debris, need for additional security measures. If patrol methods don't assure adequate coverage, they must be amended or additional lighting, alarms, CCTV installed to provide coverage from a more remote observation post.

(4) Lighting must be properly aimed to illuminate the area being observed but not to blind the security observer. The surveyor should approach the perimeter from the viewpoint of the "trespasser," noting and correcting any dead space.

c. Perimeter Barriers.

(1) Gaps or damage to perimeter fencing must be corrected. Fencing itself should be sturdy, well anchored, at least seven feet high. Strands of barbed wire or razor ribbon should add an additional foot and be angled *outward.*

(2) Unauthorized perimeter openings (damaged fences, soil erosion, exposed drainage ditches) must be corrected. Unauthorized fence

openings, like paths to the fence, may indicate employees' unauthorized use of these openings.

(3) If buildings form part of the perimeter barrier, windows accessible from the ground must be secured or sealed and protected by grills, mesh or special glass to deter damage. Exterior doors or gates must be sturdy and provided with locking devices to assure as effective a deterrent as the fence itself.

(4) Gates must be limited to the minimum number necessary for effective and safe emergency operations and, again, must be as secure as the fence itself (height, locks, proper closing, etc.) and protected (lighting, alarms, CCTV, security patrols, padlocked). The best perimeter barriers are ineffective if entrances through them are not secured.

(5) Perimeter alarms should be adequate in type, numbers, installation for their expected use and must be properly monitored with scheduled (and effective) weekly testing. Adequate security guard response to a triggered alarm is as important as the alarm itself.

(6) Perimeter lighting must be adequate, effective, properly aimed to provide proper coverage. The surveyor must test all lighting systems at night and be alert for any burned out or missing bulbs or other malfunctions. Lights should provide overlapping coverage so that a single burned out bulb will not leave part of the perimeter in darkness. This also would be a good time for him to check the adequacy of reporting procedures for correcting lighting deficiencies. The best lighting system is of little value if inoperable bulbs or switches have not been replaced.

(7) If the facility relies upon CCTV for perimeter coverage, cameras must be adequate in number, coverage, quality. Lighting must be adequate for the cameras used. Cameras must be monitored and there must be a response capability. Blind spots in camera coverage must be corrected by additional equipment or by adjusting existing cameras.

Area/Building Security

All outdoor areas of the facility must be clear of undergrowth, debris or other obstacles to clear observation or which might provide concealment. All must be readily accessible to emergency equipment.

Parking lots must be adequate; appropriately sited (near parking areas, direct flow of traffic from access gates, etc.); supported by adequate signage; properly protected by fencing, lighting, security patrols, CCTV.

The facility's traffic pattern must be realistic, providing the fastest and most direct routes possible.

Building doors opening on the facility's perimeter should be lockable when not in use or not protected by other security measures. The surveyor should check all lockable doors. Should they be locked? Are locks adequate and appropriate (expensive lock on easily forced door)? He also should insure that managers, in their zeal for better operations, have not violated fire or safety codes by improperly locked doors. All perimeter doors must be afforded lighting adequate for monitoring and/or identification checks by Security Officers or CCTV.

All vaults and safes in use must adequately protect their particular contents (burglar and fire protection). Appropriate and current opening and closing records must be maintained. The security surveyor should assess the number of people holding the combination to safes and vaults (criteria of authorized to know and need to know) and the protection those individuals give the combinations they hold.

He must check all exterior windows (or interior doors and windows to sensitive areas), particularly exterior windows accessible from the ground or from other structures, to be sure they are properly protected against intrusion or damage. Mesh, safety glass, security glazing may be used where appropriate as protection. Appropriate windows and skylights openings must be alarmed and easy access to them from outside denied.

Alarm response systems must be tested during all shifts. All alarm systems need emergency power backup not easily vulnerable to sabotage.

Security patrols of buildings and other critical areas will be especially critical during the strike. The surveyor should examine them carefully, particularly in light of operational changes during the strike, to assure they provide coverage, observation, response capability.

Lighting

The security surveyor must rate the adequacy of lighting systems, paying particular attention to parking lots, loading or receiving docks, warehouses, other particularly sensitive areas. Light at vehicle or pedestrian check points must be bright enough and properly aimed to assure good identification capability, effective CCTV coverage, overlapping coverage if some bulbs do not light.

Light fixtures must be protected against vandalism and have emergency backup power. Independently powered, portable spotlights should be available for emergency use during the strike.

The surveyor must check lighting *at night* for proper aiming of lights, brightness, blind spots, overlapping beams, nonoperating equipment and procedures for reporting and correcting those problems.

Alarm Systems

All areas and operations that should be alarmed should be given adequate and appropriate alarm protection to include emergency backup power supplies.

An alarm system can only alert the security force to a potential problem. The capability of that security force to respond quickly and effectively to a triggered alarm also must be tested. This probably will involve pre-testing coordination with the contracted alarm company or with local police.

The surveyor should do a physical audit of the current contract with the alarm company serving his facility to determine that all billed equipment and systems are present and operating properly as necessary. Often he'll find unnecessary alarms—systems installed before use of the area changed and no longer appropriate or needed. His survey is likely to correct systems and thereby affect savings that will handle his own pay for many months to come.

At least weekly, alarm systems should be tested with reports of these testings, and of all unauthorized alarm openings, reviewed by the appropriate security supervisor.

Key Control

Perhaps the greatest weakness to most physical security systems is inadequate key control—too many master keys float among unauthorized individuals. Locks are not changed when an individual leaves a sensitive area or operation and no longer requires access. Keys are issued as a convenience to users where the availability of a very limited number of master keys, under control of the security staff, would be as efficient and far more secure.

The surveyor must check all locking devices and the openings they protect. Often he'll find an expensive and secure lock, for example, on a totally inadequate, easily forced door.

The surveyor also must check the master key box at the security station to assure that it adequately protects the keys in it and that it adequately accounts for all keys at all times.

Vault and safe combinations must be afforded protection suitable to those containers' use. It does no good to have an expensive, secure safe if its combination is known to unauthorized individuals. Combinations should not be given out as a convenience to selected individuals but only to those who are authorized to handle the highest level material protected in that safe or vault and who have a genuine need to have the combination to do their jobs.

Closed Circuit Television

The security surveyor must evaluate the adequacy of CCTV coverage of sensitive areas and operations. Lighting (protected by emergency backup power) must be adequate for the television camera being used. Cameras should be provided with tilt/zoom/pan capabilities, be properly aimed, be equipped (where appropriate) with time lapse taping capability. Cameras, like lights, must be protected from sabotage or mischief (spray painting lens openings, thrown objects, theft, etc.).

Like alarms, the CCTV system can only alert the security force to potential problems. It takes a response capability to resolve those problems. The surveyor should test that response.

Often an expensive and complex CCTV security monitoring system is completely wasted because no one is assigned to monitor that camera or because monitoring systems are poorly designed. If the monitoring Security Officer is not trained, equipped, properly motivated to monitor the information his camera provides, his is a wasted effort. Often he faces conflicting duties (responding to telephone calls, processing messengers or visitors, etc.) which preclude his recognizing what his camera is trying to tell him. The effort is wasted—at great cost.

Complete CCTV monitoring logs should be maintained by all shifts and be reviewed by a security staff supervisor.

The condition of existing cameras, provisions for portable camera coverage, adequate lighting for special cameras, timeliness and quality of CCTV equipment repair are all valid concerns in strike planning.

Personnel Identification and Control

Use of personnel identification cards is of critical concern to the security surveyor. Are cards properly authorized, prepared, issued, recovered when no longer needed? Is ID card production equipment properly safeguarded?

The surveyor must consider whether special identification cards would be appropriate during a strike. If so, how will they be handled?

During a strike it is especially important that visitors be properly screened, identified, documented by the security staff and that they be escorted at all times on the facility. Security Officers are inclined to become lax in consistently enforcing these measures. That laxness must not be tolerated, particularly during a strike.

The surveyor also should measure employees' attitudes toward the identification card system and toward visitor control. Are strangers challenged by employees in work areas? Do employees habitually wear their ID badges on their outer garments at work? If the answer to both questions is, "No," the identification card and visitor control systems are of limited value and there may be need for special security orientations and for enforcement of company rules, as well as possible changes to those procedures.

Entrances/Exits

Access controls at all entrances and exits are critical to securing a facility during a strike emergency. Traffic, both vehicular and pedestrian, must be properly controlled, examined, routed.

The surveyor must be particularly alert for unauthorized entrances and exits (*e.g.*, gaps in perimeter fencing, use of fire emergency doors, etc.) habitually used by employees. If they use them during normal periods, they'll be apt to use them for unauthorized access during a strike.

Changes in entrance and exit procedures planned for the strike emergency must be assessed in terms of appropriateness, realism, effectiveness. General management will be concerned with the operational effectiveness of these emergency procedures. The Security Director must insure that they provide adequate security. He'll not only be concerned, for example, that traffic routing patterns get an individual from the front gate to his assigned parking lot as quickly and as safely as possible but also that that route and parking lot are properly lit, properly marked, properly secured.

Security Guard Force

A senior, highly experienced, mature security staff member should evaluate the company's security staffs' functions, particularly those of the security guard force.

He should review the contract for contract guards to insure that the Security Director is aware of any contractual problems that might arise in a strike situation or of contract Security Officers who might not be available during a strike emergency because of legal limitations or other commitments (off-duty policemen, firemen, etc.). He should be able to accurately brief the Security Director on increased charges levied by the contract guard company for "stand-by" guards, reserve forces, guards required to remain on the premises for twelve-hour shifts or throughout the strike. He also should insure that the Security Operations Center will have adequate telephone listings (including "beeper" numbers) and names for key contract security supervisors.

His review of contract security guard coverage should include an assessment of uniforms and equipment available through the contract guard company—hence any additional requirements that should be considered in strike control planning.

The surveyor must weigh the training of individual guard force members, proprietary and contract, and their individual capabilities as they influence individual assignments during a strike emergency. For example, individuals known to react poorly under stress, as in losing control of their tempers when faced with personal abuse, threats, physical confrontations, should not be assigned to most likely confrontation points. If it appears to the surveyor that the shift supervisors have not properly considered all these factors, he should call the supervisors' attention to them. There will be enough problems during a strike emergency without encouraging others by having the wrong individual in the wrong place at the wrong time.

If some facility guards are armed, some not, it's a good idea to use armed guards inside the facility if possible, rather than at likely confrontation points. It also is a good idea to use contract guards rather than proprietary guards for shows of force or other operations where physical confrontations are likely.

Not only should existing security department equipment be checked for proper maintenance and serviceability but also any new or additional equipment leased or purchased for the strike emergency should be checked for serviceability and for compatibility with existing equipment. If additional radios, for example, do not communicate with existing radios, they will be of limited value unless placed in a separate net of their own. This also is an excellent time to assess the adequacy of stockpiles of expendable supplies (batteries, film, etc.). Once a strike begins it may be difficult to replace or restock certain items.

The surveyor also should review existing guard rounds, post orders and emergency plans to insure that they properly support changes to operations and the physical configuration of the facility because of the strike.

The surveyor must determine that the Security Control Center, which will handle all security guard operations during the strike, is adequately staffed and equipped to handle the increased size of the security staff and the changes to its operational commitments and resources.

Report procedures probably will change during the strike. The security survey should consider whether present procedures and report forms are adequate. If they are not, the surveyor should recommend necessary changes.

The guard force probably will remain within the struck facility throughout the strike—at least its proprietary component. In any stressful situation, but particularly during a prolonged strike, facilities must be available to the individual Security Officer for dining, rest, bathing, recreation, contact with his family, clean uniforms and other required services. These would be legitimate concerns for the security surveyor.

Fire Prevention and Protection

The surveyor must review existing fire prevention and protection procedures for adequacy, currency, completeness in view of changing facility requirements during a strike. His review should include currency of tests of those procedures. If they've not had a fire drill in many months and a strike is possible, it's a good time to run an exercise testing personnel and equipment.

Alarms, sprinkler systems, extinguishers, hose systems should all be checked for suitability, adequacy, maintenance. Better to find problems now than to need some part of the fire fighting system and find that it does not work. Additional extinguishers or other equipment may be necessary to cover areas put into temporary use during the strike.

As the surveyors inspect all of the company's facilities, they should be alert for fire hazards (debris, combustible material, poor wiring, blocked sprinklers, blocked fire exits, etc.) and immediately report them so necessary corrections can be made.

Security of Proprietary Information

The surveyor should review written procedures and present practices for safeguarding sensitive company information from unauthorized disclosure or from destruction. Normally this precaution might be directed toward attempts by individuals not employed by the company to gain sensitive company information. During a strike, however, employees themselves may wish to gain sensitive information (*e.g.,* strike plans, guard deployment, company bargaining strategy, etc.). It may be necessary to alter existing procedures, such as user codes for EDP operations, to accommodate this new and unusual requirement.

His pre-strike security survey might include evaluating the effectiveness of secure emergency communications procedures, as in supervisors' telephone notification nets. This can be very critical during a strike.

His survey should include safeguarding of computer facilities and sensitive computer-stored company data. Not only must the physical security of the data center and its contained information be considered, but also the secure storage of critical backup information off-site should anything happen to the basic data bank at the struck facility.

Procedures for safeguarding and controlling access to classified company documents also must be reviewed in terms of the strike situation. Combinations of safes and lock cabinets known to many individuals may have to be changed as an interim measure with new access rosters to be determined.

Purchasing

During a strike emergency companies tend to loosen purchasing and accountability procedures in the name of expediency. This is necessary in some cases, but not always. And always it should be controlled as much as possible. The Security Director bears great responsibility for assuring that additional material or equipment purchased or leased for a strike emergency is purchased properly, directed to the right individuals, properly accounted for.

Purchase orders should be printed on unalterable paper, numbered, properly secured before use and filed after use. Purchased material must be adequately and safely stored to preclude its being damaged, misused, stolen. Inventory procedures should be examined closely, to include proper follow-up action on noted discrepancies.

Shipping/Receiving

The surveyor must review existing shipping and receiving procedures to determine areas of greatest vulnerability during a strike. He must assess loading docks' organization, physical configuration, lighting, alarm systems, security guard coverage, records, housekeeping, control of drivers and other shipping and receiving personnel. In pre-strike planning he must insure that appropriate individuals are aware of the necessity to coordinate all shipping and receiving with the Security Operations Center.

If company drivers are to be used during a strike, he might have their supervisors be certain that all are properly licensed and fully briefed on proper conduct when crossing picket lines.

Special lighting, alarms, CCTV coverage of shipping and receiving areas generated by the strike situation and beyond those normally employed in those areas should be thoroughly checked. For example, use of additional trailers parked near loading docks to provide extra storage facilities, may require special coverage.

His survey also should include security requirements at any off-site shipping and receiving marshalling areas.

Property Control Procedures

Property in facilities that will not be occupied during the strike must be secured from damage, misuse, theft. The surveyor must review existing property control measures and determine whether new or additional steps are necessary because of the pending strike.

Sensitive company property, vulnerable to sabotage (fuel tanks, pumps, vehicles, power equipment, etc.) must be given special protection.

Pre-strike security surveys also must consider handling of waste material. Will contractors be allowed on premises during the strike to remove garbage and waste or salvage material? If so, how will they be controlled? If not, how will waste material be stored pending movement off-site? If any contaminated material is involved, are storage facilities safe and secure?

It is likely that property or material passes will not be used often during a strike. Working employees should not be carrying out bundles at that time and Security Officers can do without the distraction of package inspections. If employees are allowed to remove property, however, the surveyor should determine any changes necessary to the existing material control system, such as authorization to sign building passes or designation of one gate only for removal of such material.

Vehicle Control Procedures

Proper vehicle control procedures, important any time, are especially critical during a strike emergency not only to insure proper dispatch and receiving of vehicles at the struck facility but also to assure proper documentation of vehicle and driver should both be involved in a strike-related incident resulting in legal actions.

Vehicles entering or leaving the struck facility should be thoroughly identified and logged in appropriate vehicle control logs. Guards must be instructed to identify drivers, firms, vehicles involved. Trucks carrying shipments from the facility must be inspected for obvious safety defects, seals, proper dispatch documentation. Drivers must carry necessary operator's permits for the vehicles they are operating.

Mail and Parcel Post

Routine mail procedures at the struck facility probably will change drastically with the strike. The surveyor must evaluate physical security measures for the company's postal facility, particularly if it is to be closed during the strike. He also must consider secure handling of mail delivered to the facility while normally assigned company postal handlers are absent and special requirements if the company is required to pick up mail at the local post office.

CHAPTER 9

ACCESS CONTROLS

The strikers' best tactic is to withhold their own labor while discouraging other persons from entering the struck premises and supplies, raw material, finished products from moving in or out.

If persuasion or intimidation doesn't work, they'll probably try to physically block premises access. The law doesn't allow that, but it probably is exactly what will happen until some counterforce prevents it.

The counterforce most likely is court-ordered local police action. Before that can happen, however, the Security Director must commit his own resources to deter the mass picketing and violence that would close his gates. If that does not work, he then must take other steps to document the need for court sanctions.

His early actions include choosing the gates to be used for premises access during the strike. At first glance it might seem better to dilute the picketers' strength by operating as many gates as possible, forcing more extended picket coverage. That, however, does not work out well.

Although the pickets' lines may be stretched, there will be bad side effects. The number of confrontation points and likely spots for violence increase with every gate used. Even if union leaders want to prevent violence, the more gates they must cover, the less their control over picketing strikers.

And the Security Director will have far less control over his own resources. He has the advantage of operating from interior lines, but even so he has just so many people and so much technical equipment to cover every likely hot spot. The more he dilutes either people or resources the less effective will be his defenses. His communications and control problems also are increased in direct proportion to the number of gates he must cover.

The same argument applies to local police. They will be very limited in numbers and capability. The fewer gates they must protect, the better their chance of protecting them well.

The basic rule for planning access to a struck facility is to use the fewest entries necessary to keep the facility operating.

Selected entries should be those in which loss of control by local police will create a public traffic and public safety problem. The more imminent the threat to the general public, as opposed to problems facing only the parties in the labor dispute, the faster and better local law enforcement agencies will respond. Local officials sometimes think that confrontations between labor and management are "in-house" or "family" problems. When violence touches the general public, however, it can't be ignored. The Security Director should select gates which, if interrupted by mass picketing or other measures, can cause severe public traffic problems, physical risks to passing vehicular or pedestrian traffic and possible damage to nearby private property.

Vehicle gates must be of adequate size. Non-striking employees and truck drivers, bringing supplies and raw material into the plant or carrying finished products from it, will be crossing picket lines where they certainly will be subject to verbal abuse, taunts and provocations that will distract their attention. Pickets may have erected barriers or thrown debris on roadways. There may be physical confrontations where strikers throw themselves in front of vehicles, pound the sides and windows of vehicles, or throw rocks or other missiles at them. Pickets may attempt to rock or overturn vehicles attempting to cross their lines. All this would be bad enough anytime but, if the gate is barely large enough to admit a vehicle, during a strike there is far more chance of its being blocked or of a driver's hitting a barrier or the gate or some individual on the picket line, any of which could trigger a violent reaction.

There also should be adequate room around the gate for local police to park vehicles, to erect their own traffic control barriers, to maneuver crowd control teams.

Gate signs should be clearly visible and worded as required by state and local laws. Signs should clearly designate gate use: vehicle, pedestrian, contractors only. Other signs, accompanied where necessary by yellow-paint lines, fences or barriers, or other clear markings, should indicate the boundary of the company's property. They should warn that anyone who crosses that line will be trespassing company property and subject to arrest. Gate signs also should spell out check point procedures and alert drivers to traffic flow within the facility—all so that there will be minimum traffic backup at or near the perimeter gate.

No member of the company's security force should be outside the perimeter unless an emergency requires their being ordered to help local police who are being assaulted outside the gate. Their job is to protect the facility's interior; let local police handle everything outside its perimeter.

Vehicular gates and nearby fencing should be reinforced with additional barriers and with additional floodlighting. Lighting must permit use of movie and video cameras. If no suitable vantage points for camera operators are available inside the gates, they must be improvised.

Picketing strikers may salt vehicular entrances with nails, tacks, broken bottles or similar devices. The Security Director must be prepared for this with nearby magnetic sweepers and with stand-by crews armed with brooms. They should not sweep beyond the access gates, however, until directed by local police to do so and only when given adequate protection by those police.

Another problem at vehicular entrances would be the abandonment or stalling of inbound vehicles. This might be done intentionally to block the entrance. It also might be unintentional, as when a driver becomes nervous or frightened by picket line activity and stalls his vehicle or simply abandons it. If the vehicle can't be started and moved promptly, regardless of whatever caused it to be stopped at the entrance, it must be towed or pushed away.

Inside the gate and near it, the Security Director should have heavy moving equipment: tractor, payloader or truck, equipped with cables or other towing means. This equipment should be padded (used tires or similar material) to minimize possible impact. Drivers should be carefully chosen for their skill as well as for their maturity and for their ability to remain calm under pressure.

Inbound vehicles that cannot be started must be pushed aside or into the perimeter as soon as their passengers disembark. Vehicles pushed or towed into the facility should be moved to a cleared buffer zone between the company boundary and the area where vehicles are parked or material stored. For most facilities, this will be just inside the boundary fence but far enough to limit damage by thrown missiles or by any other vehicle driven against the fence.

This cleared area should extend twenty to thirty yards, if possible, within the company boundary. A second line then should be established by using nylon line and stanchions (large food cans with old piping of common height and eye bolts at the top will do. Concrete poured into the cans adds weight and anchors the pipe).

The buffer zone is very important. Except for moving stalled vehicles into the facility, no one should be permitted to walk, drive, park or store materials in it. This buffer zone serves three critical purposes:

(1) It moves targets a safer distance from the picket lines.

(2) It creates a clear, well-defined area in which any person's trespass is immediately obvious.

(3) It establishes a positive line of demarcation between the facility's security police and local police.

Even if the facility has no company security force, the buffer zone is important in creating an added layer of protection.

If there is not enough space for the well-defined clear zone suggested (20–30 yards in depth), the area outside exterior walls of buildings near the perimeter should be cleared to provide at least some clearly defined buffer zone.

Police action to control picket lines will be discussed later but several points are worth mentioning now. Police control of gates may be by single patrol car or by dismounted police officers at each access gate. If police strength permits, an approach for a large struck facility might be for the local police unit to be divided into two or three dismounted squads. The first squad would be on line with and in immediate contact with the pickets who have moved to block the gate. On command, this first or lead squad splits with half the squad pivoting to the left, half the squad pivoting to the right, and advancing to force the pickets back and clear the gate area. Meanwhile, a second police squad, initially just outside the gate, moves as a reserve behind the first squad. The police commander would remain roughly centered in the gate area to control both squads.

All gates (vehicular, pedestrian, contractors, rail) not used during the strike must be locked with new, heavy duty padlocks and kept under closed circuit television surveillance or patrol rounds surveillance. Appropriate signs should indicate that the gate cannot be used and direct individuals to gates which are operating during the strike.

Checking the identification of drivers and vehicles takes place at the gate itself. Depending on the situation, this may be established as a quick, rough-check which then allows the vehicle to pass into the clear zone inside the perimeter and avoids dangerous traffic back-ups and possible picket confrontations outside the gate area.

Once the vehicle enters the gate, however, facility Security Officers must inspect it, identify its occupants as authorized to enter the facility, complete necessary vehicle log sheets, direct drivers to appropriate loading docks or parking areas.

If the struck facility is large, planning must include estimates of the work-area distribution of the anticipated work force and the assignment of internal roads and parking areas (emergency parking areas designated when appropriate) so that traffic moves from vehicular gates to assigned work areas by the fastest and most direct way. Traffic control and directional signs must be clearly worded, easily seen, in sufficient number.

If the security staff size permits, traffic officers may be assigned to expedite traffic flow and parking. Jockeying for parking space or convenient parking near work areas, especially if parked vehicles may block or impede security patrols or emergency vehicles, cannot be tolerated. Assign routes and parking areas and require all employees to comply with them, right from the start.

Assigned parking areas must be of adequate size. They must be well lit and they must be protected. Protection is afforded by assuring adequate space, by barriers to prevent damage to fencing and to guide vehicles, by marked and enforced parking stalls. Parking areas must be patrolled or under visual observation by Security Officers in fixed posts or monitoring CCTV cameras.

The Security Director must insure that written communications to non-striking employees include information on assigned access gates, measures to follow in crossing picket lines and entering those gates, identification procedures, traffic flow and parking within the facility's perimeter.

If pedestrian access can be accommodated safely, it should be considered. It is more appropriate in a metropolitan environment where local transit service affords easy transportation to the facility. In suburban or rural areas, however, pedestrian entry is unusual under normal circumstances and should not be encouraged during strike situations.

Vehicles cannot be safely left outside the facility and the company could not be responsible for damage to vehicles or occupants it cannot hope to protect in an off-site location. If violence is likely, people simply are a lot safer inside automobiles which cross the picket line then are safely parked inside the facility.

The chances of personal confrontations are far greater when antagonists are on foot and in immediate visual and physical contact with each other. The non-striking worker crossing picket lines is under great physical and emotional stress. He may confront long-time friends who now consider him a traitor to their cause. He may encounter individuals with whom he already has had disagreements and who welcome this opportunity for revenge. On foot and in the middle of an angry line of picketers, he is far more likely to say something, or to gesture, or simply to smile in such a way that it causes an angry response. This is nowhere near as likely in a slowly moving automobile, accompanied by other non-strikers, with windows closed and under the direct observation of local police.

Normally, non-striking employees should be encouraged to use vehicles to cross picket lines and to car pool whenever possible.

If non-striking employees are permitted to use pedestrian gates to enter or leave the facility, the number of gates should be held to the minimum number absolutely necessary. They should be clearly marked by appropriate signs, and employees should be notified in advance of their designated use.

Pedestrian gates should allow quick identification and passage through an outer check point with closer identification and any package inspection inside the perimeter. Foot traffic should be channeled into one-person passage, however, to preclude "piggy-backing" by which unauthorized individuals might slip into the facility and to aid the identification process.

Pedestrian gates must be well lit. This protects the individuals concerned, assists identification and inspection procedures, facilitates CCTV and camera coverage of gate activity. It may be necessary to provide extra floodlighting.

Obviously company security force and local police coverage at personnel gates is critical and must be adequate at all times but particularly during shift changes.

A basic rule in controlling safe access to a struck facility is that the number of movements past picket lines must be minimized. Leaving for lunch or periodic breaks are obvious mistakes. A strike is an emotional issue. Pickets take any movement through their lines as a defeat for their cause. To them, the intruder has chosen sides—not theirs. No matter what his reason for crossing their lines may be, he is someone to be confronted and stopped by whatever means possible. Picketers may allow an individual they know to enter at the start of a shift, to leave when the shift is over. But if that individual seems to flaunt their line by passing through it several more times during the day, they may see his excursions as contempt for their cause, as baiting. They're likely to respond violently.

If a struck facility can bring in enough of a working staff to operate in any fashion at all, it can provide food for lunch breaks without the employees having to leave the premises to eat elsewhere. During a strike, nothing is gained by a lunchtime exodus. And management is likely to lose the whole game if it permits needless excursions during breaks.

A final consideration is the inordinate burden frequent crossing of picket lines by non-striking employees places on local police who have to maintain order at the gates. They can maintain that order only by stripping their forces elsewhere or by putting a heavy overtime load on individual police officers. They won't care for that. In sum, once an employee enters the facility, let him stay there until his work is done.

Shipments in and out of the struck facility will be covered in a separate chapter. The same basic rules apply. Use the least number of gates possible (presumably this would be by the one or two vehicular gates already designated); use qualified and carefully selected drivers; schedule movements to provide the maximum protection possible to assure rapid, smooth, safe moves through picket lines; schedule as few picket line crossings as possible.

The same considerations apply for contractor gates. Security at contractor gates, however, may be more difficult to enforce. If construction or other contractor activity is to continue on a large facility during a strike, it is best to designate a specific gate for use only by contractors.

Contractor gate observation and protection should be the same for other vehicular gates. Contractor gate signs, worded as required by state or local laws, must state that that gate is to be used only by contractors.

Contractor gates must not be used by vendors or by any contracted technical specialist (alarm technician, telephone repairman, etc.). If individuals, other than contractors engaged in a specific construction project, use gates reserved for contractors only, or if these gates are used for other purposes (*e.g.,* management's attempting to use them to transport supplies or finished products), management may be guilty of an unfair labor practice and subject to severe penalties.

Contractors, union and appropriate facility supervisors, non-striking employees and local police must be notified in writing of gates designated for contractor use only. The contractor must agree, in writing, before attempting to enter the facility during a strike, that he will use only the designated contractor gate and that his employees will comply with on-site security, traffic, parking requirements.

The Security Director will find that contractors are perhaps the most difficult group to convince that they must comply with his strike control procedures. They will argue about the weight of their tools and supplies, the distances involved, the time and cost factors and the danger of a strike by their own employees if they are inconvenienced in their work. They'll argue for this exception and that exception, ostensibly to expedite their work. Each request must be considered on its own merits, but experience has shown that one-time exceptions quickly become "traditions" and that contractors do not have the facility's best interest at heart at all (certainly not the job of the Security Director) but will take advantage of every opportunity to make their own work easier at whatever expense to their client. Whatever rules the Security Director establishes, he should stick with them and enforce them until he is sure he has the strike situation under control. Then, and only then, he may be able to relax just a bit, but not much.

Generally, the most critical time of a strike is at the beginning when massive picket lines block entrances, preventing egress and ingress. This is when you need all the outside police protection you can get. If violence occurs, you must document it with moving pictures, still photos, video tape, recordings, or statements by witnesses—if you hope to win a court injunction limiting picket activities. This is especially critical during shipping and receiving operations.

Shipping and receiving security measures will be discussed later. Suffice to say, maximum police and security force coverage of these activities, and of shift changes, is critical. Film coverage of assaults on police or on non-striking employees or private citizens, resistance to arrest, attempts to overturn or damage vehicles or similar illegal picket activity, is very important. The very presence of documentary staffs and equipment, and the obvious intent of the Security Director to use them, go far to deter violence. If violence does occur, it will go far in stopping it and in preventing its happening again. This is true even if the cameras are not working or there is no film, lighting is insufficient, or observers are inexperienced in using their equipment. Strikers can't know all that. And, if they're smart, they can't afford to take the chance. They must assume that the company will have documentary evidence and will use it. Every effort at documenting or seeming to document strike activity is worth it.

The Security Director must know of any concessions or arrangements between management and the union (or individuals), allowing striking employees to enter the struck facility for any purpose. Individuals concerned should be fully identified, if possible, as should whatever they have been authorized to do. The security staff, and supervisors in work areas, must know these arrangements to reduce the chance of confrontation and to control the individuals while they are on the facility. Any special concessions, allowing striking employees to return during the strike, must be coordinated with the Security Director so he can schedule them at his own convenience, at times when there is less chance of conflicting activities, and when he can properly supervise them.

If management plans to transport individuals to or from the facility other than in their own automobiles, the Security Director should know about it. What alternate means of transportation are planned: trucks, buses, vans, helicopters, boats, rail cars? Where will employees meet outside the facility? What times? Are there any company security requirements? What schedules are planned for leaving the struck facility? Have arrangements with any contracted transport companies included compliance with his security plans? Have local police been notified? If no one has approached the Security Director about these matters, he must resolve questions on his own initiative and assure that he'll not be overlooked or by-passed in future planning.

As a general rule, car pooling should be encouraged. Alternate means of transportation, other than busing or some similar ground transportation, should not be encouraged—for example, the use of helicopters to transport workers. By the time the workers assemble some distance from the site, considerable time and effort already have been lost. And the carrying capacity of commercial helicopters makes it a questionable exercise from the standpoint of cost alone. Any mass pooling of workers, other than by surface transportation, is questionable.

Nevertheless, somewhere there is a manager or two who will decide such an approach is innovative, daring, imaginative. And he'll plan it without considering the security implications involved. The Security Director must be alert for these innovative, daring, imaginative tactics long before they are handed to him to carry out.

If visitors are to enter the facility during the strike, the Security Director must coordinate days and times involved. Anticipated visitors (as sales representatives who routinely visit the facility once or twice a week) should be notified that the facility has been struck and of any appropriate security requirements.

The Security Officer receiving visitors must be sure that the visitor register is completely and accurately completed and that the individuals and their companies are identified and verified. This deters unauthorized access and is not an unreasonable requirement.

Visitors should be permitted only when the security staff can handle them. *All* visitors must be escorted at all times when they are on the facility. If this cannot be done by a non-striking employee of the department visited, it must be done by a Security Officer or the visit should be denied.

Visitors must be issued visitors' badges and be required to wear them on their outer garments. Badges should be noted on the visitors' registers and collected at the end of the visit. Under no circumstances should a frequent visitor be allowed to keep his visitor badge or be excused from logging his visit in the appropriate register.

Visitors who fail to comply with security requirements may be counselled and/or denied further entrance to the facility. Similar disciplinary action might apply to employee escorts who fail to correct the visitor's non-compliance.

The security staff, particularly those in the Security Operations Center, will require detailed, current, accurate personnel rosters and other information concerning individuals associated with the struck facility:

(1) Rosters of salaried employees, job titles, departments, plant ID numbers including special strike ID numbers, access restrictions, vehicle license numbers, home addresses, home phone numbers, persons to be notified in case of emergency.

(2) Rosters of hourly workers, striking and non-striking, with the same information.

(3) Rosters of union officers (plant/local/international) with (as appropriate) plant job titles, departments, plant ID numbers, vehicle license numbers, home addresses, home and office (if appropriate) telephone numbers, persons to be notified in case of emergency.

(4) Rosters and similar information, as above, on any employees (striking or non-striking) who are required for special maintenance requirements and with whom special arrangements have been made for periodic visits to the facility during the strike. A copy of any written agreement should be included.

(5) Names, company addresses, telephone numbers, beeper numbers of vendors, repairmen and contractors who may be entering the facility during the strike. If certain drivers or other individuals usually represent their companies at the struck facility, include their names, positions, verifying authority at the servicing company, emergency business and home phone numbers. Rosters should be accompanied by a copy of the company's written confirmation of pledged compliance with the facility's security requirements and that its employees will cross picket lines.

The Security Director must determine which buildings and areas will be used during the strike and which will not. Those which will not be used must be protected by padlocks, by warning signs, CCTV surveillance and security force patrols.

Special consideration must be given those buildings and areas which will be used during the strike. Existing security procedures for them may have to be augmented or otherwise revised. Parking areas may have to be modified or redesignated.

In all probability shifts will be modified. Perhaps the facility will go to a twelve-hour shift. The company may require the emergency staff to remain inside the facility for the duration of the strike. Meal arrangements must be clarified. Employee time card punching procedures may have to be changed, requiring special instructions to gate guards.

Certainly package or material pass systems and requirements for inspection of vehicles and employees' packages will tighten. For instance, during the emergency who will be authorized to sign and issue property passes?

The Personnel Department must supply the Security Director with samples of employee identification cards normally used and with samples of special identification cards to be valid during the strike. The Security Director should review security aspects of processing these special identification cards to include the security of processing equipment, authorization to sign and/or issue the special identification cards, security of completed cards and return of cards when the labor dispute ends.

As special identification cards are issued to employees, the Security Operations Center's roster of these individuals must be amended and a sample of the special cards made available for use there.

During a labor dispute special emphasis must be given to requiring all employees on the facility, from executive to janitor, to wear their company identification cards on their outer garments at all times.

The Security Director also must tighten procedures for checking incoming and outgoing vehicles. He will coordinate this requirement with the company's legal staff and with other appropriate managers. The company's requirements for inspection of vehicles entering or leaving the struck facility must be conveyed, in writing, to all individuals and other companies likely to enter or leave the facility during the strike. This will be covered in more detail in the discussion of shipping and receiving.

Access controls are meant to deny entrance to the facility to unauthorized individuals and to facilitate the apprehension of those who may be able to breach its perimeter.

Unless strikers are maintenance specialists periodically returning to a struck facility, by agreement between the union and management to perform necessary repetitive maintenance functions, such strikers are not *bona fide* employees once a strike begins. If found on company property after a strike is declared, they should be considered trespassers. This is a valid concern in access control planning.

The Security Director should determine his facility's boundaries and be certain that they are if necessary clearly marked by signs, fencing and paint. The signs must clearly convey the idea that the area within that boundary is company property and that trespassers will be prosecuted. He also should make certain that those boundaries are clearly delineated in the company's early written communications with the union and with individual employees.

Once that is done, any striking employees found on company property are trespassing and likely to be arrested. As the company and its representatives have no power of arrest, the security staff can only detain the individual until the arrival of local police who, upon complaint of the company, would make a valid arrest.

In the end, prosecution probably would depend upon the particular situation and upon the individual involved. The employee with an excellent work record who has stolen back into his former work area to clean out his personal locker will not be treated like the one caught opening a drainage valve to flood an area with diesel fuel or attempting to sabotage a transformer.

The basic principle, however, is that the company, as represented by the Security Director and his staff, must establish rules to maintain order and prevent or deter illegal acts during the labor dispute. Once established, those rules should be enforced.

A final consideration for the Security Director planning access controls, but one which always must be on his mind, is the logistics and cost involved in any security operation. That will be covered in detail later, but the point is that much as he might like to surround the facility with a wall of steel, equip his staff with all the latest electronic wizardry, and perhaps increase that staff four-fold, he just can't do it. It would cost too much. Most of the additional equipment might never be used again. And he'll never have total security anyway. In total security, nothing moves and nothing happens. That can't apply to a business. So the Security Director must be mindful of costs and always open to alternatives by which he still can accomplish his mission.

CHAPTER 10

SHIPPING AND RECEIVING

I f the inclination to use too many access gates during strikes is the most vexing problem facing the Security Director, perhaps the second most troublesome would be management's insistence on shipments to and from the struck facility that are of no real consequence.

The employer clearly has the right to receive and ship goods during a strike, but if the movement of raw material and supplies into the facility can't be followed by the production and shipment of finished products out again, the exercise is of little value, and it can be dangerous. Shipping and receiving operations during a strike provide perhaps the most likely situations for confrontation and violence.

If shipping and receiving during strikes are important, however, or if they must be accomplished to demonstrate "business as usual," the Security Director must try to insure that they are done under the best conditions possible: when local police can support the facility's security staff, when picket lines can be crossed smoothly and quickly, when trucks and drivers' exposure to harm are least. It can be done, but to do it well and to do it as easily as possible, the Security Director must have the cooperation of other members of the management staff.

Carriers licensed by the Interstate Commerce Commission (ICC) must pick up and deliver goods at strike-bound facilities unless there is grave risk of injury to drivers or property. Getting those companies to do it, however, may be another matter indeed. Most such carriers are operated by members of the International Brotherhood of Teamsters Union (Teamsters). Unfortunately, Teamsters have long been associated with more violent picket line clashes. Individually and collectively they do not carry a "cooperative" rating in labor disputes.

In any event, the employer should notify the carrier that he intends to use that carrier's service during the strike and that, failing to receive it, he will consider legal action against that carrier. This notification should be verbal and written and the employer should insist on a written commitment in return.

Legal actions in matters of this sort would be directed to the ICC for revocation of the carrier's operating authority; to federal district courts for damages and injunctive reliefs; to state courts for conspiracy charges and payment of damages under appropriate anti-trust laws.

Handled properly, the problem of getting common carriers to cross picket lines in receiving and delivering shipments to a struck facility can be resolved. It may be worth trying. If it works, there is significant psychological impact to those common carriers' ignoring picketing strikers to support management's operations.

Whether the company can get a large interstate carrier to support its operations or must rely on a smaller, local carrier operating from a shipment collection point outside the struck facility, the Security Director must verify certain agreements. Have truckers made firm commitments to cross picket lines? Will those truckers comply with the facility's security procedures, to include drivers' conduct while passing through picket lines?

He also should verify that all truck drivers will have proper driver's licenses and appropriate insurance coverage. If drivers of either contracted carriers or company vehicles are not properly licensed, the struck company may be liable for personal injuries or property damage resulting from the failure of those drivers to do their jobs properly.

The Security Director should discourage any management personnel who personally undertake to drive company vehicles during a strike emergency, particularly if those vehicles are large semi-trailers having to maneuver in small areas or having to cross picket lines. Invariably those managers are not experienced in handling that type vehicle or have not operated one in many years. Some can drive forward, others (a few) can back a trailer. Fewer yet have done both in recent months. The practice is dangerous to everyone concerned and can result in heavy legal and financial penalties. Be sure that a driver is licensed to operate any vehicle he is asked to drive, that his driving is properly covered by liability insurance, that he really is technically and emotionally competent to handle that vehicle in a tight place during a difficult time. Because that is what he will have to do.

If management plans to use local carriers or company vehicles and drivers for shipment into or out of the struck facility, the Security Director must know details of this arrangement. Will small trucks or vans be used? Will they be company or leased vehicles? What kind? What schedules have been established? Will his security staff and local police resources be able to accommodate that schedule? Will any of the trucks be carrying hazardous materials: gasoline, oil, solvents, other chemicals? If so, will they require any special security or other arrangements?

In pre-strike meetings or, if necessary, early in the strike itself, the Security Director must convince union leaders that all persons and vehicles have the right to enter and leave the struck facility at will and that police officers are obliged to enforce this right.

Perhaps the best way to handle drivers attempting to bring shipments into or out of the facility is for the police to allow one person—a union official or picket captain—to talk with the vehicle's driver. This should be done in the presence of a police officer and while the vehicle is parked off the street where it will not impede normal traffic.

The strikers' representative may tell a truck driver that picketers are on strike and have established a picket line. He should be given reasonable time to try to persuade the driver not to cross the picket line. The police officer merely listens; he must not advise the driver whether to cross the line or not. All he might do is tell the driver that he can enter the gate or not enter it, but that that decision must be the driver's alone. If necessary, he might add that the driver will be given no police protection on the way out but that the picket line will be cleared and the driver protected while he is entering or leaving the struck facility.

If the driver decides to enter the facility, the police officer should ask the picket captain or union representative to clear his pickets from the path of the vehicle. If, after a reasonable time, the gate has not been cleared, the police commander may attempt to negotiate with the union's chief representative or may simply direct local police squads to open the lines. Local police probably will open the picket lines only far enough to allow the vehicle to enter the gate area, then allow it to reform so long as pickets keep moving and do not permanently block the passage of foot or vehicle traffic.

When picket lines are forced open by police action, police officers should face the picketers rather than the persons or vehicles entering the gate. This allows them to watch the actions of the pickets and deters pickets' threats to drivers or damage to trucks or other property. Facing the pickets at all times also allows police officers to identify any individuals involved in illegal acts during the vehicle's passage.

If the picket line is small, the police officer's cautioning, "Watch the cars," probably will be sufficient. He must be cautious in using hand signals, however, because a wave of his hand may be interpreted as *directing* the vehicle to enter the struck facility.

Similar problems develop for rail shipments at a struck facility. Railroads clearly are involved in interstate commerce. They must complete deliveries to a struck plant; they must take out contracted shipments. That's federal law. Sometimes, however, this creates misunderstandings and bad feelings between local police or railroad police and union representatives because the union will charge that law enforcement is being partial to both management and to the railroad.

An approach to this problem is for the railroad representative to notify local police, management and labor representatives in advance of a scheduled shipment. Special agents of the railroad and local police officers then will be present at the railhead servicing the struck facility. If railroad crews, being union members, refuse to cross the picket line at the railhead, a *supervisory* train crew will replace them.

At this time the local police commander informs the picket captain that the train is about to enter the facility. He'll then request that pickets clear the railroad tracks. If they refuse, he will cause local police to clear picket lines. Pickets normally will be given reasonable time to consider their position and to shift their lines before they are forced to do so. Picket lines should be cleared only enough to allow the train to pass into the facility. Further clearing of pickets from railroad property adjacent to the tracks would be the responsibility of railroad police.

The Security Director or his representative should be present during rail movements into or from the struck facility, and the rail gate should be under observation, from within the perimeter, by the company security force.

If the facility plans rail shipments, the Security Director should know the scheduling as far in advance as possible. He also might suggest that the transportation supervisor assure that spare hoses, valves, wrenches, and other special equipment for use with tank cars, are available in case they are needed so that rail activities won't be delayed.

In addition to hindering truck shipments through picket lines, a fairly common strike tactic is for strikers' cars to follow trucks leaving the struck facility and attempt to intimidate drivers away from the premises. This can be particularly troublesome and dangerous because the intimidation may not occur until the truck is far from local protection. Local law enforcement agencies will have to handle that problem.

It is best to establish a marshalling point some distance from the struck facility. At this marshalling point shipments to and from the company may be reloaded and transhipped. Protection to and from this intermediate point usually is easier to assure, particularly if routes to it follow well-traveled highways which are frequently patroled by municipal, county or state police.

Outbound shipments are transferred to local or interstate carriers from this marshalling point. Their dispersal, perhaps in several vehicles, none particularly identified with the struck employer, can make further pursuit or harassment impractical.

Inbound shipments are handled the same way. Interstate carriers drop off shipments at the marshalling point. Here they are concentrated, reloaded on local carriers, and moved (under protection if necessary) into the facility at scheduled times when they can be given the most protection at the picket lines.

Management must advise all suppliers to ship to this alternate location and assure their willingness to do so. If this causes security concerns, they must be coordinated with the Security Director.

It probably will be necessary to establish this off-site marshalling point around leased warehousing, again not obviously related to the struck employer. The company may provide contract guard security and, in a prolonged strike, may consider periodically moving the marshalling activity to other locations. The Security Director must constantly monitor the security of operations at the off-site marshalling point.

The Security Operations Center must be alerted to all scheduled shipments into or from the struck facility so the Security Director can arrange maximum security force strength at contested gates, the presence of Observation and Documentation teams to witness picket activity, and the presence of local police outside the facility.

Additional warehousing or storage areas may be necessary *within* the struck facility to accommodate reserve supplies or product storage resulting from more limited shipping. Extra trailers may be parked near docking facilities if those dock areas can't handle the extra capacity. In these cases, the Security Director must consider any additional security requirements (padlocks, lighting, CCTV coverage, patrols, etc.).

During a strike, additional company or leased vehicles may be stored on the facility. Will they require additional or different parking areas and additional security protection? The Security Director should know whether scheduled maintenance on these and other company vehicles will be performed on-site or at local garages and how it will be scheduled.

No matter where scheduled maintenance is to take place, maintenance supervisors should assure that an adequate supply of additional vehicles and spare parts are on-site for emergency use.

The Security Director also must know of plans for waste and salvage pickup. Have disposal company drivers agreed to cross picket lines? Are those drivers licensed and qualified? Have they also agreed to comply with the facility's strike plans (parking areas, traffic control measures, etc.)? Have arrangements been made for spotting extra waste containers around the facility? What changes will all this require to existing security procedures? Except for the last item, these considerations are not the primary concern of the Security Director. He should be alert to them, however, in pre-strike coordination with other managers and to security-related problems that may develop from them during the strike.

Shipping and receiving can create severe problems for the Security Director. By understanding and anticipating those problems, however, he can plan around them, assure necessary coordination by other staff members, direct measures to ease those problems.

CHAPTER 11

LOGISTICS

Logistics concerns during a strike are not the primary responsibility of the Security Director, but he must acquire equipment and supplies he will need to carry out the Security Department's functions and he will be concerned with security aspects of logistics management.

One of his primary concerns will be the logistics support of employees who will remain in the facility during the strike.

Some individuals probably will remain on-site at all times. Most will be there only during the work day but some (supervisors, maintenance technicians) will be there overnight, all or part of the time. Those who stay overnight must be quartered. That means cots, bedding, lockers, shower facilities. They must be on hand before the strike deadline. The emergency staff will need laundry services too. Will there be pickups and deliveries or will laundry be done off-site? If done on-site, who will do it and how many employees will be involved? These factors and requirements for controlling laundry vendors must be considered as additional security requirements.

Provisions for uniforms, clothing, toilet articles, towels, soap and other personal comfort items also affect security planning. Will they be stock piled or will they require additional vendor access? If they're to be stored on-site, they must be safeguarded.

Dining arrangements pose special problems. The Security Director must consider the number and type of meals to be served each day. Where will they be served and at what times? For how many people? Will meals be prepared on-site or brought into the struck facility? How many employees or vendors will that involve? Will those workers remain on-site or will they cross picket lines each day? The answers to these questions suggest problems in safeguarding food and dining facilities and more people-control situations, particularly in frequent picket line crossings.

Recreational activities for the emergency staff remaining on-site during the strike pose additional security problems. These could mean additional vendors crossing picket lines. If special recreational equipment (radios, televisions, video games, etc.) is to be leased or purchased, it must be secured or some time during the strike situation some of it will walk away.

Routine mail and parcel post handling procedures probably will be altered to some extent during the strike. If the company normally picks up its mail at the local post office, how will that service be handled during the strike? Will that pose additional security problems, as in the storage of undistributed items and in crossing picket lines several times a day?

If temporary general headquarters for the struck company is to be established off-site during the strike, will interoffice mail delivery into the struck facility create problems? Will the temporary headquarters require special security precautions to discourage attempts to interrupt its operations?

New telephone, telex, computer lines almost certainly will be required in a prolonged strike. The Security Director will be concerned about additional communications' security problems their use generates. He'll also be concerned with proper handling of any central telephone switchboard at the struck facility. Can communications to the emergency operations centers be established and maintained? Can sensitive operations centers and conference areas periodically be swept for hidden electronic listening devices? Will those areas require any special access controls?

Housekeeping procedures surely will be affected by the strike. Vendors entering and leaving the struck facility pose special control problems. The Security Director must know the approximate times vendors will be operating and in which areas; almost as important, he'll need to know the buildings and areas previously serviced but which will not be serviced during the strike. If they contain vending machines or sensitive equipment, they must be protected.

Companies contracting to handle waste and salvage disposal may continue to cross picket lines during the strike. If so, certain questions must be resolved. How will their schedules be affected? Are additional dumpsters or other trash receptacles planned? Where will they be spotted? If non-security supervisors routinely check trash bins and other waste storage for possible theft of company property, how will this function be handled during the strike? Will the security staff have to assume this responsibility? Will garbage be picked up on a regular basis? If not, what problems will this cause for the security staff?

Once the Security Director knows how logistics managers intend to provide all these services, he can plan to meet the security problems these arrangements create.

Stockpiling of raw materials is another pre-strike operation of interest to the Security Director. Will stock piles be complete before the strike begins? If the strike is prolonged, what resupply of raw material and supplies will be necessary? Will it be by rail, truck, tank truck, boat? Have any schedules been established? Although raw materials, fuels and lubricants, packaging material, etc., are not the responsibility of the Security Director, their receipt, storage, distribution, accountability may affect his operations.

Spare parts and stockpiled supplies might include the following:
- a. Vehicle spare parts: rotors, plugs, tires, points, etc.
- b. Boiler room chemicals for oil and water treatment.
- c. Pumps, fittings, hoses.
- d. Hard hats, respirators, gloves, safety supplies.
- e. Steel, lumber.
- f. Packaging material.
- g. Gasoline and lubricants.
- h. Solvents.
- i. Oxygen, welding supplies.
- j. Toilet tissue, paper towels, soap, industrial cleansers.
- k. Uniforms, rainwear, boots.
- l. Emergency tire inflators.

Some of these items might require additional or special storage areas and additional security against fire, theft, other loss or damage.

The Security Director should review security aspects of planned emergency purchasing and contracting procedures. What recurring purchasing is expected? Do purchasing agents understand the need to coordinate their activities with the Security Operations Center on such matters as shipping, receiving, transport security? What instructions have been given to sales representatives likely to plan to visit the struck facility?

The Security Department should have a blank purchase order capability. Needed security equipment and supplies must be on hand before the strike deadline but invariably there will be new or additional requirements. In those instances the Security Director may not be able to wait for routine handling of purchases. If verbal purchase requests have been authorized, the Security Director should know about them. Who has that verbal purchase order authority? What are its limitations? This is part of his normal concern for possible theft or misuse of company property. Lines of accountability can become slack during a company emergency; his job is to keep them as taut as possible at all times.

The Security Director should discuss routine maintenance scheduling and handling with responsible company managers. If some striking employees will enter the facility during the strike to handle boiler room maintenance or other technical requirements, who are those individuals? What will be their maintenance schedules and where will they be working? Has all this been coordinated with the union to preclude problems at the picket lines?

Routine maintenance on vehicles, forklifts, tractors and similar heavy equipment should be current before the strike begins. Breakdowns will occur, however, during the strike. How will they be handled? Has the maintenance supervisor been instructed to coordinate off-site requirements with the Security Operations Center?

There will be many logistics requirements that directly affect the Security Department—such as specific items required for security activities during the strike:

a. Additional lock cylinders for changing facility locks for which there are numerous unauthorized keys floating about.

b. Portable traffic barriers.

c. Special signs: traffic, directional, gate use, trespassing, identification check point procedures, etc.

d. Security transport vehicles to move Security Officer teams to critical areas.

e. Vehicles to house and transport Observation and Documentation Teams.

f. Bolt cutters for removing improper padlocks, chains or wiring.

g. Magnetic sweeper devices to sweep gate areas of nails, tacks, other devices placed to damage vehicle tires.

h. Heavy duty tow trucks, front end loaders or tractor type vehicles for removal of vehicles stalled in critical gate or road areas.

i. Supplies and equipment for the Security Operations Center, such as:

(1) Typewriters, desks, chairs, bulletin boards, file cabinets, safes.

(2) Office copy machines and supplies.

(3) Paper shredders.

(4) Office supplies: paper, pencils, pens, acetate, paper clips, thumb tacks, hole punches, grease pencils, etc.

(5) Large maps, schematics, aerial photos of the struck facility for pinpointing problem areas and directing security activities.

(6) Blueprints, schematics, photographs of individual buildings/areas for deployment of security guards and other measures.

(7) Flashlights; emergency office lighting.

(8) Foul weather gear.

(9) Special telephone hookups for conference calls and for direct access outside the struck facility.

(10) Telephone recording equipment.

(11) Portable heaters or air conditioners, as appropriate.

(12) Commercial television sets for operations centers.

(13) Good quality video cassette recorders with batteries.

(14) CB radio for monitoring pickets' and emergency agency communications.

(15) 8 mm movie projector.

(16) Slide cassettes with screen.

(17) Base radio to control any security staff radio nets not already covered by the base station at the Security Control Center.

(18) First aid supplies.

(19) Emergency rations.

(20) Movie cameras, 8 mm, with ample supplies of film and batteries.

(21) Cameras, 35 mm, with ample supplies of film and batteries.

(22) Mobile television cameras with necessary power packs, batteries, etc.

(23) Additional FM walkie-talkie radios for use by Observation and Documentation Teams, additional Security Officers, special requirements. Radios should have multifrequency capability or be selected with a mix of several frequencies for various security teams. Equipment should include ample supplies of spare radios, extra batteries, recharging units.

(24) Paging (beeper) devices for key members of security staff.

(25) Night vision equipment with adaptors for camera and TV use.

(26) Tape recorders with ample supplies of extra recorders, batteries, extension cord, tape. Recorders should be large enough to pick up picket line sounds with some recorders of smaller size for interviews, investigations, on-the-spot reports.

(27) Portable loudspeakers with an ample supply of spare batteries or alternate power sources.

(28) Portable floodlights with electrical wire or provision for battery use; ample supplies of bulbs, batteries.

(29) Additional permanent floodlights, mounted in gate areas and at other critical points.

Additional logistics concerns might be management's plans for keeping facility streets and sidewalks clear during snow emergencies, emergency power and lighting systems, emergency rations.

The Security Director must be sure that the facility designated for the Security Operations Center is adequate in size and equipment and suitable to handle the normal three to four man staff. Immediately adjacent should be additional office space for the Security Director, for other individuals, for conference rooms.

Supplies and equipment purchased during a strike emergency are apt to be received and issued to individuals or departments without being inventoried, checked or marked as company property. Standard procedures come loose during crises. Supply records become more informal, less accurate under the pressure of the moment. The Security Director must do all he can to insure that all supplies and property are used as they were meant to be used, are properly accounted for and are returned when no longer needed.

CHAPTER 12

EMERGENCY OPERATIONS CENTERS

In a strike situation normal lines of command and control are not adequate. Strike problems are not normal problems. Key executives' attention is focused on collective bargaining to end the labor dispute. Normally that bargaining will take place away from the struck facility. So individuals who normally would make day-by-day decisions about company operations probably will not be available during a strike emergency. Some managers may find that they have no clear-cut "normal" functions to perform. Curtailed operations alter their responsibilities. Sometimes this leads to serious management problems because those usually busy executives may look elsewhere to expend their energies and authority, often to bad effect. Toes are pinched, command and control lines become snarled.

The company's chief executive should designate a temporary emergency staff to handle day-by-day company affairs within the struck facility while he and other executives work from less restricted headquarters on the collective bargaining process and on long range company problems. He assigns responsibilities within the operating units and delegates authority, normally to the managers or functional heads of those operating units, to meet those responsibilities.

If a company has done its pre-strike homework, that means authority and responsibility to carry out specific plans and contingency options already spelled out in the company's overall strike management plan.

The Security Director, for example, should be given authority and responsibility to implement the Security Annex to operations planning. He'll be responsible for facility access, picket line disturbances, protection of all company property, police liaison, documentation of unlawful conduct, fire prevention.

The company often will establish two basic groups or teams. One—call it the General Planning Group—will occupy an office area established as a General Operations Center. It will include carefully selected management and supervisory officials of unquestioned maturity, experience and loyalty to the company. They'll be supported by a small clerical staff. From the General Operations Center they'll be responsible for overall management strike tactics and for production, public relations, shipping and receiving, medical support, logistics.

The second group, headed by the Security Director and comprised entirely of security staff personnel or other individuals temporarily assigned to the security staff, will operate from a separate Security Operations Center.

The two groups are physically and operationally separated, but both operate twenty-four hours a day, seven days a week, during the strike. They must meet at at least once every day, and they must keep each other informed of all strike matters as they develop.

To avoid confusion and misdirection, however, the Security Director or his representative should give no commands to any member of the General Operations Group and no one except the Security Director should give directions to the security staff.

All information concerning the strike, all questions from the news media or others, all scheduling of non-security related activities, should be funneled through the General Operations Center whose staff will then coordinate with the Security Operations Center.

The Security Operations Center, established during emergency situations such as labor disputes, should not be confused with the Security Control Center. The Security Control Center is a permanent headquarters which also operates twenty-four hours a day, seven days a week, not only during emergency periods but at all times. It controls routine daily activities of the security guard force and security clerical staffs. It monitors special electronic equipment: fire and intrusion detection and alarm systems, CCTV security surveillance. It maintains Security Officers' shift reports or other routine Security Department reports.

The Security Control Center is a busy place at all times. Its extensive electronic equipment is permanently installed and constantly monitored. It will continue to function during a strike emergency but during that time comes under the control of the temporary Security Operations Center.

The Security Operations Center will maintain all reports and other documentary evidence concerning the strike. These could include:

    a. Security Control Center logs and reports.

    b. Security Operations Center logs and reports.

    c. Investigative reports.

d. Observation and Documentation teams reports.

e. Photographers' reports (still, movie, video).

f. Audio tapes and reports.

g. Incident reports.

h. Reports of witness' interviews and affidavits.

The Security Operations Center staff must report and investigate all strike-related incidents, both inside and outside the facility, concerning work stoppages; sabotage or other damage to property; violence; disorder.

They must coordinate physical security measures, as during shipping and receiving operations, with the General Operations Center, with company supervisors, with the security staff.

They must coordinate company liaison with municipal, county and state police or with other court or law enforcement agencies or special police (rail, water).

They must handle any unusual security requirements in areas of lighting, gates, fences, etc., and coordinate their monitoring with the Security Control Center.

They must operate a continuous information gathering service for strike-related matters: photographs, video and movie film, still photos, audio tape recordings, newspaper clippings. They must insure that this information is constantly in an organized format for use by the staff of the General Operations Center which has final responsibility for overall company policy, including public relations efforts.

The journals of the Security Operations Center and Daily Operations Summaries prepared by the Security Director must give management a clear and current picture of the strike situation. These daily reports might include the following:

a. Time the picket line was established, discontinued or resumed.

b. The number of pickets each hour with significant changes in numbers noted.

c. Names of pickets; changes in picket line strategy; other significant data concerning picket lines.

d. The number of non-striking employees, management and non-management, present for work in the struck facility during each shift.

e. Specific picket line incidents.

f. The presence or absence of union leaders, local or national. The presence or absence of signs, loudspeakers, weapons, barricades on the picket lines.

g. If practicable, the names of non-striking employees going through the picket lines and problems they encountered. If numbers are large, summaries of employees' experiences.

   h. Complete identification and analysis of all Incident Reports, photographs or other visual or audio documentation, affidavits or statements of witnesses concerning incidents which took place during that twenty-four hour period.

   i. Reports of any meetings between the Security Director or a security staff member and striking employees or with law enforcement agencies, public officials.

   j. Summary of all communications between the General Operations Center and the Security Operations Center, other facility managers. This is an activities report, not a statistical summary.

   k. Reports of significant facility operations (shipping and receiving, personnel actions, production) during the reported period.

Obviously this much detailed information should be submitted only when it is physically possible and reasonable to do so. There is no point, for example, in submitting lists of more than fifteen or twenty employees' crossing the picket lines. What the Security Director is trying to do is to convey an accurate impression of general strike activity at the time.

The reports should clearly and thoroughly document any unfair or illegal practices by striking employees. On the other hand, if strikers are picketing peaceably and abiding by their pre-strike agreements, that too should be noted. It's the fair thing to do and, should that daily report be needed as evidence in a legal proceeding, its impartiality will strengthen its acceptability and credibility.

Reports will be covered in more detail in a later chapter, but several points are worth mentioning now. All records of picket line or other work stoppage activity, including photographs or video/audio tapes, are strictly confidential. That's one reason for physically separating the General Operations Center and the Security Operations Center from other employees, including executives, who may be in the facility during the strike. Reports and other documentary evidence should not be released from company control without the express permission of the company's chief executive, on advice of his legal counsel.

The Security Operations Center should be established in a facility office which is easily identifiable and convenient to reach. It helps if it is fairly near (and hopefully able to observe) the most likely point of conflict during a strike (*e.g.*, main vehicle gate) but must be distant enough so as not to be subject to risk during a violent confrontation. It must be adequately secured at all times.

The Security Operations Center must be large enough for a continuing staff of three or four individuals and the equipment cited below. It should be adequately heated or cooled, as appropriate, and adequately lit. Emergency electrical power for lights and other equipment must be readily available.

If such an area is not available in an existing physical structure, it may be necessary to rent an office trailer to use as the Security Operations Center.

The Security Director should personally select individuals to man the Security Operations Center and personally prepare formal written guidance for them. If at all possible, he also should personally conduct oral briefings for all key members of his staff during the strike crisis.

Individuals manning the Security Operations Center should be well versed in all security matters and should be mature, discrete, capable of using sound judgment in taking action on their own without close guidance. They should know the company's operations and should be thoroughly familiar with the physical layout of the facility and with any off-site operations (as in marshalling points for shipping and receiving activities).

The Security Operations Center staff will control the company's security force, through the Security Control Center, and will personally direct all operations of Observation and Documentation teams, picket line testers, investigators. Some of these individuals, as investigators or Observation and Documentation team members, may be operating outside the facility during the entire strike but must maintain close contact with the Security Operations Center for direction and guidance.

Of particular concern will be investigation, analysis and supporting documentation of any Incident Reports. Incident Reports may be submitted to the Security Operations Center by anyone, security or non-security staff, employees or non-employees. They might report the following:

a. Threatening or obscene phone calls at the facility or at employees' homes.

b. Bomb threats.

c. Damage to company property or to employees' property.

d. Objects thrown at company property or at employees' passing near picket lines; other acts of intimidation, sabotage, vandalism.

The Security Operations Center must have immediate access to current and accurate rosters:

a. Supervisory personnel, employees, proprietary security staff, contract security staff: names, departments, plant identification card numbers, home addresses, home telephone numbers, business telephone numbers (if appropriate), vehicle identifications to include license numbers.

b. Contractors and vendors: companies, primary contacts, telephone numbers, addresses, vehicle identifications.

c. Union seniority lists, union officials: names, positions (within the union/at the facility), plant identification card numbers, home and office phone numbers, vehicle identifications.

d. Office and home telephone numbers, business addresses, names of primary contacts for the following:

(1) Local police.

(2) County Sheriff.

(3) State police.

(4) Rail or other special police.

(5) Hospitals, doctors on call, emergency teams.

(6) Bomb disposal units.

(7) Fire.

(8) Contract guard company (including "beeper" numbers).

(9) Contract video or alarm maintenance services (including "beeper" numbers).

(10) Film processing or other logistics support companies.

e. If possible, extra company personnel identification cards and/or personnel photographs.

The General Operations Center and the Security Operations Center, as well as any conference rooms to be used for strike strategy planning, must be physically secured with periodic electronic sweeps conducted of rooms and associated telephone equipment to preclude unauthorized disclosure of sensitive information. For the same reason, records of both Operations Centers should be secured at all times. Staffs must be periodically warned of the confidential nature of anything they observe or hear while participating in strike control measures.

Staffs of the General Operations Center and the Security Operations Center must constantly exchange information and coordinate planned activities. Success or failure of strike management measures largely depends on how well these groups work together.

The Security Director must see that individuals selected for the Security Operations Center are well qualified by experience, maturity, temperament and loyalty. He should personally prepare written staff guidance and conduct periodic briefings to be sure that everyone still is marching to the same drummer. He should be physically present during much of the first seventy-two hours of a strike. After that, his staff should be trained and ready to handle events as they occur. In his absence, however, he still must be readily available for consultation on any major decisions. In the end, it's his responsibility anyway, and that just can't be delegated.

CHAPTER 13

OBSERVATION AND DOCUMENTATION TEAMS

The union and the workers it lawfully represents have the right to picket during a labor dispute, to tell persons that a strike is on and to urge them not to cross their picket lines, so long as they do it peacefully and without threats or acts of violence.

The company must respect the employees' right to carry on peaceful picketing. In turn, however, the company lawfully expects the union and striking employees to respect its right to operate its facilities safely and without damage and to assure the free access of employees and visitors, supplies, raw materials, finished products.

During a strike, special teams of carefully selected supervisory and/or security staff employees, working under the supervision of the Security Director or his representatives manning the Security Operations Center, are charged with recognizing and documenting all strikers' activities which are unlawful or which involve disorder or violence. Documentation may be by photographs, movie camera, television, audio tapes supplemented by first-hand accounts of witnesses and their own reports.

This documentation is useful in three ways:

a. To support criminal charges or suits for damages.

b. To support disciplining or terminating employees for illegal strike activity.

c. To support application for injunctive relief.

The overt presence of Observation and Documentation teams is very effective in discouraging violence or other improper or unlawful strike activity. Even if actual documentary evidence is not taken. The perceived threat that it *may* be taken often is enough to discourage striking picketers from behaving in a disorderly or unlawful manner.

Use of Observation and Documentation teams, however, can be a two-edged sword. Their presence, with documentation equipment, can incite anger and confrontation. In addition, court decisions have held that documentary surveillance of workers engaged in legitimate strike activities, such as legal picketing during a lawful strike, can itself amount to an unfair labor practice by management in that it interferes with the workers' lawful exercise of their rights. For these reasons, Observation and Documentation teams should *not* photograph or video tape *peaceful* picketing activities. These would be described in the teams' hourly reports but would not be photographed.

Because of the sensitivity of their mission, because team members risk confrontation with striking picketers (and will have to live with those fellow employees long after the labor dispute ends), because the company itself risks an unfair labor practice charge if the team uses poor judgment, team members must be carefully selected. Then they must be trained to use documentary equipment. Most important, they must be trained to recognize activities which should be documented and those which should not.

Team members must be capable of operating without close supervision when necessary but should have fairly close supervision whenever possible. Guidance in difficult situations must always be nearby.

Observation and Documentation team members should be of supervisory or management level, of recognized maturity, judgment and ability. They should know the hourly work force well and be able to talk with its pickets if necessary. Hopefully, they will have long experience with the company and enjoy the trust and confidence of other employees. Under no circumstances should they be individuals symbolic to the labor dispute at issue and whose very presence is likely to cause confrontation and violence. Each team leader must be a particularly competent individual who can make quick and accurate decisions on what and how to document an event.

Team members must know the facility and its operations well. If they also know the picketers, especially those in leadership positions, it eases problems of identification in reporting incidents.

Separate from the Observation and Documentation teams, but similar in some respects to them, are supervisory or management level employees selected as picket line testers. Their job, at the onset of the strike and periodically as the situation develops, is simply to pass through picket lines and then to report their experience. It is a way for management to determine problems other line crossers are likely to encounter. Picket line testers would not remain near the pickets during the strike, as do Observation and Documentation team members, but simply would pass through picket lines enroute to or from their work areas.

Picket line testers must be thoroughly briefed beforehand on what to expect from pickets and how they should conduct themselves when crossing picket lines. The briefing might include the following cautions:

a. At all times use great care passing through the picket lines.

b. If police officers are on duty at the entrance gates, follow their directions.

c. Use turn indicators each time you enter or leave the facility.

d. Ignore any verbal or visual abuse from the pickets. As you drive past the pickets, concentrate on the proper and safe operation of your vehicle. Keep windows closed. Do not exchange words or gestures with pickets. Any comments or gestures from pickets, no matter how personal or vulgar, must be scrupulously ignored. Failure to do so would only worsen strike conditions. Remain cool, calm, patient. Gradually work your car through the line. Do not run into anyone. Do not use force. Do not cause a confrontation.

e. Remember that you have the right to free access to and from company facilities at all times. If pickets refuse to let you pass, sound your horn until you have adequate room to drive through. This also will serve to notify plant Security Officers and local police that you need help. If this does not work, retreat. Call the company for further help or guidance. Once you are away from the picket line and can safely park your car, make notes on what happened. Include the date, time, gate, names of individuals concerned, what you heard and observed.

f. If nails are spread over the roadway, do *not* drive over them. Report it to the local police and to a company Security Officer. The driveway will be swept.

g. While passing through picket lines, if you realize that your car has been or is being damaged by the pickets, continue until you are clear of the line. Then inspect for damage and report it to local police and to a company Security Officer. If you can identify the individuals responsible, do so. The last thing you should do is to stop your car, dismount and get into a fight, verbal or physical, with the pickets. The company can repair your car or replace it; it can't repair or replace you.

h. Report each instance of threats, damage to property (your vehicle, your home, company property) and other serious incidents to local police and to company security.

i. Car pool as much as possible, even if only for the last few miles. If the company has not arranged a marshalling area outside the plant to secure parked employee vehicles, be sure you leave them far from picket activity. Inside the plant, park your automobile in designated parking areas only.

j. Plan to stay in the plant during your entire shift. Unless you are notified otherwise, food will be provided. If an emergency requires your leaving before your shift ends, have your supervisor notify the Security Operations Center.

k. If you feel you cannot abide by this guidance, particularly as it pertains to your conduct while passing through picket lines, please say so right away so that some adjustment can be made.

Picket line testers have a difficult and potentially risky job. They are the first to cross lines manned by nervous, inexperienced, perhaps frightened and probably angry fellow employees who feel that strike action is the only way they can win their goals. Those strikers also believe that those who are not with them on the picket line have chosen to join the other side of the dispute. "They're for us or against us," is the accepted judgment.

It's a risky job. Picket line testers must be exceptionally mature, low-keyed, thick-skinned (or at least able to give that impression) individuals who can think on their feet and foresee the consequences, short and long-lived, of the wrong word, the wrong gesture, the wrong facial expression in the wrong place at the wrong time. They also must be alert and have good memories for faces, names, things they see and hear. Their reports, taken soon after they cross picket lines and enter the struck facility, may have great affect in establishing the tone, direction, duration of the strike.

Picket line testers must be debriefed by the security staff, perhaps with other managers present. Their reports will be carefully weighed in determining management's response to initial picket line tactics.

Because of the difficult and demanding nature of their job and the personal hazards (physical danger, threat to individuals or their families, prospect of long and bitter relations with other employees), the company should use managers, supervisors or security staff members to do as much of the picket line testing as possible. These individuals are experienced in working with others and usually are older and more mature than the average individual. Besides, that's the kind of thing they're paid to do. Use them, at least at the very start, when possible.

Pre-strike planning must include the selection of individuals for Observation and Documentation teams and assignment of specific teams to critical areas. Teams may have to switch locations to cover an unexpected point of conflict or to back another team at a critical gate, but essentially they should work one area. That way they can become familiar with that area and determine the best vantage points to cover it.

They normally are located within the struck premises and far enough back to avoid physical contact with strikers. In large facilities they probably will be located in or near vehicles which provide shelter as well as transportation for quick deployment. If high-rise buildings are near the perimeter, teams may be stationed on their roofs or in windows. It's fine if they are clearly visible to strikers. Their presence will do much to cool enthusiasm for violence. Just keep them out of range and not subject to charges of "baiting" strikers.

Each team should be equipped with two-way radios on a special Observation and Documentation team net monitored by the net's base station in the Security Operations Center. If sufficient two-way radios are not available, telephone check-ins may be used. Radios, however, are much better. Incidents worth documenting flare up with little or no warning and may burn for only a moment. Teams doubtful about action they should take, must have immediate guidance.

Observation and Documentation teams, as with the rest of the security organization and probably with the entire emergency staff, should operate on twelve-hour shifts: 0600–1800, 1800–0800 hours, daily, unless otherwise directed by the Security Operations Center.

The Security Operations Center, or an individual designated to command all Observation and Documentation teams during that shift, would control periodic team breaks, using a reserve team to spell the others. When teams are not actually documenting illegal or disorderly activity, they remain watchful. At the start and end of their shifts they should report to the Security Operations Center for briefing and debriefing and to submit necessary reports.

Observation and Documentation teams should be equipped with still cameras (35 mm), with motion picture cameras (8 mm), or with portable video cameras with sound recording capability; and with tape recorders.

Before beginning their duties, all team members must be thoroughly trained and tested in using all assigned equipment. It is far better to "waste" a roll or two of film, a handfull of flash bulbs, a hundred feet of video tape in practice than to fail to document a critical incident because an individual did not know how to use the equipment or discovered too late that the equipment itself was faulty. If teams have practiced with their equipment, they'll use it with confidence in a real situation and probably do a good job with it.

Observation and Documentation teams must have plenty of film, bulbs, spare batteries, special lens and other accoutrements with them at all times. Spare equipment and extra supplies also should be readily available in the Security Operations Center.

Depending on the nature and severity of incidents documented and time requirements, film can be accumulated for processing at intervals. Time, however, always is the critical element, not costs. For that reason it's better to remove a film magazine with only 30–40 feet exposed than to lose hours or days waiting for the whole roll to be used and processed.

In pre-strike preparations, film developing means should be established on the facility, if possible, to include training non-striking employees to handle film processing. If film can't be developed on-site, the Security Director should arrange for commercial companies to expedite processing during the strike. Color film may have to be forsaken to expedite processing. If so, black and white film will do nicely. The aim is clear, complete, accurate documentation without undue concern for other artistic requirements. Unless an instant print camera is used, two (2) copies of each print should be made.

If a group of strikers commit a violent or clearly illegal act very early in the strike (the time it is most likely to occur), and must quickly confront photographic or video evidence of that act, it can have a very real dampening effect on future strike tactics.

Observation and Documentation teams must be assigned or have immediately available Blazers or other vehicular transportation. They're needed for rapid deployment. They're also good for on-station shelter during bad weather and at night. Lights in team vehicles should be turned off from dusk to dawn.

The Security Director's orientation to Observation and Documentation personnel should cover their duties, their conduct with strikers, security staff matters.

Team members are to be alert for, observe, photograph or otherwise document every incident which involves mass picketing, violence, intimidation, damage to property.

More specifically, they should note and document such activities as the following:

a. Strikers' palming or concealing in their sleeves sharp objects which then are scraped along the sides of vehicles passing through a bunched picket group. Sometimes flat rocks or metal plates are used in the same way to fracture glass windows or headlights.

b. Strikers' scattering tacks or sharpened devices on the road or in entrances to cause flat tires. Childrens' jacks with filed points have been used this way. Nails have been similarly used after "pretzel folding" in a vise. Often the items are slipped through a hole in the trouser pocket.

c. Strikers' lock-step picketing to cause a continuous barrier which does not allow passage through the line.

d. Strikers' falling or lying in front of vehicles or in entrance ways. This often is combined with feigned injuries from an alleged accident.

e. Strikers' inciting to riot or encouraging a breach of the peace through specific, inflammatory words or actions (including use of placards or other signs).

f. Strikers' abandoning a motor vehicle or deliberately blocking a thoroughfare. Letting air out of tires. Frequently a car is driven to or through a gate and then deliberately stalled.

g. Strikers' putting sugar in vehicle gas tanks, cutting ignition wires, breaking into parked cars or trucks.

h. Strikers' hurling stones or other missiles or explosives at the struck premises or at non-striking employees or police.

i. Strikers' carrying, making, using unlawful weapons such as slingshots, billy clubs, switch-blade knives, etc.

j. Strikers' assaulting non-strikers or police officers from the crowd or when the assaulted person's attention is directed elsewhere.

k. Intimidation, as when pickets stop cars or employees and forcibly prevent their going through the picket line, pull employees from cars, overturn cars, or break car windows.

Observation and Documentation teams, particularly during shift changes, also should be alert to note and report the following activities:

a. Picketing.

    (1) How many pickets are at the gate at various hours?

    (2) How many feet apart are they walking? Shoulder to shoulder or how?

    (3) Do pickets move out of the way to allow cars or personnel to pass, or do they stall clearing a path?

    (4) Are pickets stopping cars to talk with occupants?

(5) When they talk with occupants, do they seem to attempt to intimidate occupants by voice, gestures, other overt threats?

(6) Are pickets causing traffic jams?

(7) Are pickets following employees' cars from the facility?

(8) Are pickets following company shipments from the facility?

(9) Names, identifications, activities of strikers.

(10) Names, identifications, activities of strike leaders. Who are picket captains?

b. Weapons.

(1) Watch for any weapons: clubs, pick handles, rocks, nails, slingshots, can openers, etc. Photograph them.

(2) Are these weapons used in any unlawful acts, as described above?

c. Nearby Groups.

(1) Watch for groups of persons not actually picketing but standing around, observing.

(2) Are they relief pickets?

(3) Have they any weapons? Identify individuals and weapons if possible.

(4) What seems to be their purpose?

(5) What is their outward attitude? How do they display that attitude?

d. Common Carriers.

(1) Watch for trucks which pickets turn back.

(2) Get the license number, name of truck line, time of any incidents involving trucks and drivers attempting to enter or leave the facility.

(3) Watch for attitudes of pickets and truck drivers. Identify individuals who seem unusually belligerent and apt to cause problems in the future.

e. Incidents Involving Employees Entering or Leaving the Struck Facility.

(1) Watch for and record times, car licenses, identifications of car occupants, conduct of pickets, attitude of pickets and vehicle occupants if unusual, possible conflicts.

(2) Note and identify employees (striking and nonstriking) who are belligerent or otherwise potential sources of trouble.

f. Signs.

Watch for and make note of various picket signs, placards, handouts.

g. Language of Pickets.

Is it boisterous, abusive, offensive, disorderly, insulting, threatening?

h. Performance by Proprietary and Contract Guards.

Are they observant and performing duties properly? Are any individuals displaying an attitude likely to cause confrontation with pickets? Report problems immediately to the Security Operations Center and note in shift report.

i. Performance by Local Police.

(1) How many police are present?
(2) What equipment are they using?
(3) What is their attitude toward the pickets?
(4) What is their attitude toward company activity?
(5) Identify individual police officers or strikers' vehicles.

j. Observe, Identify, Report to Nearest Security Officer Post
Any Observed Trespassers on Company Property.

Keep the individual(s) in sight and witness the Security Officers' handling of the situation.

k. Note Visitors.

Direct them to the appropriate guard post and continue to observe them until a Security Officer has them under control. All visitors must be escorted at all times when on company property.

l. Note and Report Any Actions By Local Citizens, News Media, others outside the company property but who are not associated with the strikers.

Do their actions favor one side or the other in the labor dispute? Why do they seem that way?

m. Other Activity.

Note and report strikers' use of sound trucks, megaphones, radios, etc. In these cases, identify the leaders and their activity.

Still photos or video tapes should document injured persons, damage to company property or facilities, any unusual incidents on the picket line which could lead to violence, injury, or blocked access to company premises. If feasible, tape recordings should be made of sounds accompanying these incidents.

Referencing data should be recorded by the observer on video tapes or tape recordings describing the incident. The authenticating data is necessary to completely identify the filming, to describe the incident, and to provide details that may be necessary later if observers must testify about those incidents.

For example, video or tape recordings might be introduced as follows: "This is John Jones, leader of O/D Team #3. With me are William Brown and Joe Smith. We are on the roof of Building #1 facing and about 60 feet from Gate #1. It is 0735 hours, July 15, 1984. There are no obstructions between us and the gate and nothing to block our view of that area. Weather is clear, visibility good. The picket line in front of Gate #1 has grown to about fifty pickets and they now have closed the gate. Several company employees are attempting to enter but have been blocked by pickets. One employee is Roy Green; can't identify the others. Pickets are arguing with local police. We recognize Sam Thomas and Bob Brown among them. We now film this activity." Team members would continue with written or oral (taped) notes as the situation permits.

After the activity is filmed, they will prepare an Incident Report on it, fully describing what happened, who saw it happen, who caused it to happen. The Incident Report will be crossreferenced to the video, movie, still photo or audio tape evidence. When the team prepares its team journal it again will cross-reference that entry to its Incident Report and to its documentary evidence. Still photos, as they are developed, must be cross-referenced on the backs of the prints to the incident. For example:

Taken by _____   O/D Team # _____

Date   _____   Time   _____

Place   _____

                 _____

Number of Photograph _____

Incident Report #   _____

Summary of Activity   _____

                 _____

                 _____

Rubber stamps with this essential data should be available to Observation and Documentation teams.

Reports and records will be discussed in detail in a later chapter. It's worth saying at this point, however, that an improper or illegal incident witnessed by Observation and Documentation teams and properly documented has a good chance of not being risked again. Team documentation may be used in prosecuting criminal charges against individuals or in civil suits against the union. It also may be needed for disciplinary action against individual employees. This may occur days, weeks, even months after the incident occurred.

Observation and Documentation team members therefore must make complete, accurate, legible notes during or soon after the incident occurs; document the incident as throughly and as well as possible (video, still photo, tape recorder, witness statements, etc.); identify documentation for cross-referencing; complete written reports for the record. If an incident occurs on a shift, team members observing that incident should not leave the facility or go off duty before submitting complete written reports about it. As soon as film or other documentary evidence has been processed, that evidence should be crossreferenced to those team reports. Don't wait. Too much is happening. Human memory is too fragile. Affixing responsibility is critical to maintaining order in the labor dispute.

Observation and Documentation teams must maintain strike logs documenting activities noted during their shifts. If nothing unusual happens, they'll indicate that too. Log entries would be of those things already discussed. More specifics on report writing are included in a later chapter. The basic rule, however, is that logs and other reports should be clear, concise, simple, accurate. They should state facts or clearly identify any hear-say reports.

Members of Observation and Documentation teams are exposed to very sensitive information about the strike. They will be aware of management's plans and security measures. They will see picket or other strike activity which the company may not wish to have released to the general public. After all, the company and its employees are going to live with that community for a long time after the strike is settled. Observation and Documentation team members must not answer any questions by the news media but should refer them to the General Operations Center. They also must not discuss any incidents, reports, procedures, directives, or any other strike-related information with anyone outside the Security Operations Center.

A final note on Observation and Documentation team operations: The team leader is responsible for all company property used by his team. That includes all equipment and all supplies. Whenever possible, he should personally sign for it. He should insure that serial numbers are correct and that all items are present. If they become broken, lost or damaged during strike operations, he should report that to the Security Operations Center as soon as possible. In training his team or in assuring adequate documentation of all incidents, he should use all the film or other supplies he needs. Better to waste a few rolls of film than to miss documenting a critical incident. Neither, however, should he waste those supplies. When the operation is over, he should gather equipment and remaining supplies (film, tapes, batteries, flashlights, etc.) from his team members and see that they are properly returned to the Security Operations Center.

The significance of detailed and accurate documentation of illegal or improper strike activities can't be overemphasized. Noting, reporting, substantiating these incidents is critical to good strike management strategy and to proper legal action, as in defending against unjustified unemployment compensation claims, supporting criminal prosecutions, or in arbitration to end the strike.

CHAPTER 14

SECURITY GUARDS

The security guard force is the infantry which will protect the facility's perimeter and interior. It is fortunate if that force is proprietary—that is employee Security Officers—or if it can provide necessary supervisors for a mix of proprietary and contract Security Officers.

Security Officers recruited, trained, equipped, led by the Security Director and his key representatives should be far more effective than contract agency Security Officers. Individual selections should have been far better. Background investigations and performance evaluations should have winnowed out unsuitable individuals. Training should have been far more extensive and more professional that that offered by a security guard agency. Proprietary Security Officers also should be better disciplined and better motivated because their jobs offer more incentive and security and should mean more to them. Going into a strike situation, a proprietary security force also should be better prepared for having worked under established standing operating procedures at the struck facility, rather than for numerous clients in many different environments. If the Security Director has done his job, he's fortunate to have his own in-house force rather than having to rely on a contract guard agency.

It doesn't always work that way. He may have no proprietary security force at all. In a strike situation he may have to rely on "deputizing" supervisory and non-striking employees to form a very informal and loosely controlled patrol of the facility. This type group can't hope to enforce the law adequately or to stop individuals determined to damage the facility. If they are lucky, they can only detect these individuals' presence and watch them until local police arrive. They are well intentioned but simply are not qualified by training, motivation or strength to do much more. Very early the company would have to turn to a contract guard agency.

In another situation the company may have a proprietary security

130

force adequate in normal times but inadequate during a prolonged labor dispute.

The Security Director can stretch the capability of his proprietary force by several measures. Before the strike deadline arrives, all security personnel except a limited number who may be required outside the facility (*e.g.,* Security Officers protecting off-site facilities, investigators), should be required to report to the facility, prepared to stay there until the labor crisis ends. Vacations would be canceled. Individuals are of no help if they can't get into the facility or if their arrival is delayed. When they are needed, they must be available. That means being quartered on-site until the strike ends.

The Security Director also could extend shifts to twelve hours' duration: 0600–1800, 1800–0800 hours, daily. Elimination of the third shift provides augmentation for the other two shifts and a ready reserve for emergencies. If the entire security force can't be kept on-site at all times, the longer shifts will allow maximum manpower during peak activity periods (*e.g.,* shift changes) and a reserve or response force.

In most strike situations, however, the security force becomes a mix of proprietary and contract guards. The proprietary force, in whole or in part, remain inside the facility while contract Security Officers cross picket lines at twelve-hour intervals. This works all right if the Security Director anticipates the problems he'll face in blending the two forces, carefully evaluates the worth of his contract guards and is judicious in assigning responsibilities.

If at all possible, contract security guards should work under proprietary security supervisors. If the struck company has no in-house guard supervisors, the Security Director may have to use contract guard supervisors working under the overall control of a proprietary security staff member.

Part of pre-strike planning must be the Security Director's determining the size security force he will need. If this indicates that contract guards may be necessary, he'd best start early getting them. Once the strike begins, getting them may be difficult. Some states do not allow contract guard agencies to provide guards exclusively for a strike. If that is not a local problem, another would be that contract guard agencies simply do not have a large, trained manpower pool available on short notice. They will have to drain coverage of other clients. Individuals siphoned into a strike assignment may not be well motivated. When they learn they are expected to remain inside the struck facility for twelve hour shifts, they may be considerably less motivated. And if the contract guard agency has difficulty finding privates for their ranks, it will have more difficulty locating enough well qualified supervisors.

The point is that the Security Director must plan ahead, determine security force requirements and pre-arrange contract guards' availability. He must have a firm commitment from the contract guard company to provide necessary manpower, properly equipped (to include any special equipment such as two-way radios he cannot provide himself), and properly trained. Time permitting, he or his representative should review the training and performance records of individuals to be assigned to his company and, if possible, interview the individuals or at least interview the guard supervisors.

If any proposed contract Security Officers are off-duty, moonlighting policemen, or firemen, or members of other emergency teams (medical, army national guard, etc.), they may not be available during a strike situation—certainly not for the twelve-hour shifts. If they are off-duty policemen, there also may be problems of conflict of interest in handling strikers.

The Security Director also must have a clear understanding of the costs involved. There will be actual duty time but there also may be considerable "standby" time. He should review the security agency's contract to be sure of the costs involved for his company.

The Security Director or his staff at the Security Operations Center must be able to contact key contract guard supervisors at all times. They must know who to contact in emergencies (guard dispatcher, account representative, etc.) and have those individuals' business and home telephone numbers and "beeper" numbers readily available.

The assignment of contract Security Officers to posts within the struck facility may be critical. Are there special requirements, as at gate posts, for more experienced and more mature officers? Does the contract guard agency have individuals to meet those requirements?

A basic rule worth following in security guard assignments during strikes is that the proprietary guard force should be kept well inside the facility with contract Security Officers manning its perimeter. That reduces the chance of confrontation between employee Security Officers and employee strikers. These people are going to have to live together for a long time after the basic labor dispute ends. The less bad feelings aroused by confrontations during the strike, the better. If there must be confrontations, let the contract agency personnel make them.

A word of caution, however, in that the average contract Security Officer probably will not be as competent or as motivated to the company's best interests as one the Security Director has worked with for some time. He may have to use old hands in particularly sensitive situations, regardless of the mud it may stir. It's a good idea, for example, to have two-man posts at access gates and one should be a trusted and very competent proprietary Security Officer.

If contract security guards work under the supervision of the proprietary security staff, chances are they will do all right. Whether proprietary or contract guard, each security shift must have a shift supervisor who is directly responsible for all Security Officers' performance of duty.

In a one-man post, supervision will be by roving supervisors. Supervisors of Observation and Documentation teams also can help by monitoring all Security Officers' performance and immediately notifying the Security Operations Center if there are problems.

One additional caution about planning use of security forces: In preparing for a strike, the Security Director should realize that a show of too much force by the employer could provoke a violent response from striking employees. This has legal (unfair labor practice charge) and practical consequences. The use of heavily armed guards or of guard dogs, when there has been no threat of violence, has been seen by courts as excessive shows of force which precipitated violent reactions from the strikers.

It may be necessary to supplement a guard force with trained attack dogs. If there has been a rash of sabotage attempts—trespassers who have done considerable mischief to the facility, disorders, physical damage to company property or injury to employees which local police have not been able to control—attack dogs and handlers, provided by a firm licensed and properly insured to provide that service, may be a good solution. If the dog handlers are competent and their charges well-trained, it certainly will be an attention getter to strikers. And probably a very effective deterrent. If attack dogs are used, they should be used overtly. Let there be no doubt that the dogs are there—that they are on patrol, that their handlers will use them, if necessary, to preserve order. Attack dogs must be kept on firm leash, not allowed to roam free nor released unless the handler is attacked. Properly used, they can be a very effective addition to the security force. On the negative side, of course, is the adverse publicity and bad feeling they almost certainly will generate.

All Security Officers must fully understand their jurisdictional rights and restrictions, both on and off company property. The duties, authority and responsibilities of the company's security force extend only so far as, and never beyond, the limits of company property. Even on-site they are limited in authority. If illegal acts occur on company property, the company's security force (proprietary and contract) must apprehend the perpetrators. Private Security Officers (proprietary or contract) have *no powers of arrest,* not even on their employer's property. They can only apprehend and detain the individual until local police arrive. Upon formal complaint of the company, probably through the Security Director or his representative, the police then will make the necessary arrest.

Company security forces must confine their activity to within the facility (perimeter and internal guard rounds, traffic control, fire prevention, preventing trespass). Outside the perimeter fence, adjacent streets and facility entrances are the responsibility of local police.

Security Officers should have no contact, verbal or otherwise, with strikers. They should not argue, confront, fight or harass strikers. They should not discuss strike issues. They should let others do the negotiating. They should not interfere with any picketing activity which is *off* company property unless, in an extreme emergency and upon order of the Security Director or the Security Operations Center, they are ordered to aid a police officer under attack.

Company Security Officers should not accept refreshments, such as coffee, sandwiches, candy from anyone on the picket line, nor should they offer any.

Unless a specific weapon is *authorized* and *directed* by the Security Director and, where licensing is required, the individual is properly licensed to carry that weapon, Security Officers should not carry weapons (guns, knives, brass knuckles, saps, nightsticks, chemical mace, etc.) on company property.

Company Security Officers, by their very presence, are identified as protecting their company's interests. Therefore, they must be particularly careful and self-disciplined not to allow themselves to be baited by name calling, threats, insults, abusive language or obscene gestures by anyone in the picket line.

In sum, they must remain friendly, tactful, polite, helpful but also firm, professional, completely objective. They should maintain a visible but low profile and use a firm but low-key approach in any contact with striking employees unless they are specifically ordered by the Security Director to do otherwise.

If a security supervisor is instructed to relay any information to striking employees, he should do that only through the picket captain.

Security Officers must not talk to or give information to the news media. They should politely refer all such queries to the General Operations Center.

A final point on attitude. Company Security Officers, proprietary or contract, should avoid displaying what some call a "cop mentality."

Professional policemen have a difficult job. They often are criticized, confronted, even assaulted. They seldom are praised. Sometimes they must face one or more angry and potentially dangerous individuals single-handed. To enhance their authority, they need some kind of "edge." Many seek this psychological advantage by setting great distance between themselves and all private citizens. They'll not respond to a smile. When spoken to, their response is cautious, skeptical.

In most cases, that much caution is not necessary. The average citizen pretty much obeys the law. He instinctively respects police authority and is somewhat fearful of the individual police officer. In short, every policeman may not need quite the "edge" he thinks he needs.

Private Security Officers certainly don't need it. In a strike situation, pickets are not hardened criminals, nor are they professional law breakers. For the most part they are nervous, frightened, uncertain individuals put in a position they really would rather not be in at all. They are not breaking a law by striking—not if their picketing is done in lawful manner in support of a lawful goal. They simply are using the means they think best to win goals they think they deserve.

Some of these individuals may deliberately break the law. Some may be provoked to become disorderly or to damage company property. But usually they have no intention of harming anyone or of seriously harming their company. After all, it's their livelihood. The Security Officer should approach them with firmness but with objectivity, never with a "there's them and there's us" attitude.

When the strike ends, labor and management must become reconciled. The less unnecessary bad feelings during the strike the better. The approach of the individual Security Officer, seen as managements' representative, can go far in that reconciliation process.

If Security Officers already are well grounded in their field, no real additional training is required for strike management. A thorough orientation by the Security Director is critical, however, as is close supervision by shift supervisors. Security Officers must understand the role of Observation and Documentation teams and their orientation also should include a review of illegal or improper picket activities, as discussed earlier.

Because coordination among Security Officers, Observation and Documentation teams, and the Security Control Center, is so important, radios must be used properly.

Radio transmissions must be limited to operational requirements. They must be clear, concise, accurate. Individuals must be trained to think out their messages before they begin to transmit. Only one individual can transmit on a particular communications net at a time. With many radios on the same net, each transmission must be important. Otherwise it may cut out more important traffic. If it isn't important, it should be delayed until the net is free. The base station must enforce communications discipline, including reminding individuals that all radio transmissions can be monitored by individuals outside the security force and sensitive information disclosed to unauthorized persons.

Security forces patrol and post orders may have to be modified by strike conditions. New ones may be necessary for additional strike coverage.

During patrol rounds, Security Officers should inspect perimeter fencing for damage and possible trespass (holes in fence, covering over barbed wire, holes under fence, etc.). They must check gates, doors, windows. They must report all broken windows, inoperable lights, leaks, spills and other fire, safety, security hazards.

If patrolling Security Officers note any illegal or unusual activities, they should report them to the nearest Observation and Documentation team and to the Security Operations Center. The Observation and Documentation team can move to cover that activity while the Security Operations Center provides guidance in handling the situation.

Security Officers must be disciplined never to leave their assigned posts until properly relieved. If an emergency requires their unscheduled relief, they should be in radio or telephone contact with their shift supervisor or with the Security Operations Center. No post should be left uncovered unless the Security Operations Center directs it.

The security force must know how to handle visitors. Normal visitor controls may be changed during the strike. Visitors may be allowed only on certain days and at certain hours. Special visitor identification badges probably will be used during the strike. Visitor identification and verification, sign-in and sign-out procedures and escort control are especially critical during a strike.

When a visitor arrives, he should be escorted from the entrance gate to the security post where his visit will be processed. He should be required to provide personal and company identification. Unless both identifications are clearly valid, the Security Officer should call the visitor's company and verify the individual's identity.

This data and other required information, covered later under "Reports," must be entered in the visitors' register. Immediately after those entries are made, the Security Officer should verify their accuracy and completeness. He must be polite and tactful but very professional. If entries have not been properly made, the Security Officer should require that they be corrected before the visitor can enter the facility. He then must notify the department or individual being visited and arrange for someone to escort that visitor at all times. He should see that proper safety equipment is issued to and worn by the visitor and that the visitor's identification badge is fixed to that individual's outer garment where it is clearly visible. When his visit ends, the visitor must return that equipment and sign-out in the visitors' register.

During a strike, the company probably will use special individual identification badges for non-striking employees. Security Officers must be alert to insure that those identification badges are worn by *all* employees from the time they enter the facility until they leave. If an individual cannot produce a valid identification badge, the Security Officer should ask for other identification (*e.g.*, driver's license to be compared with personnel rosters) to verify the individual's employee status. Then, unless the security staff have been given blanket instructions on handling this type situation, the Security Officer should contact the Security Operations Center for guidance. Employee access rosters should be available at security posts manning access gates.

Security Officers are responsible for deterring violence; they must not encourage it in any way. They should not carry weapons unless specifically authorized and directed by the Security Director to do so. And they *cannot* use physical force against an individual unless it is absolutely necessary to protect themselves from physical harm or to prevent imminent loss of company property. The security staff should avoid any show of force unless it is specifically authorized and directed by the Security Director. In those cases, it is best to let contract security agency personnel demonstrate that force rather than the proprietary security staff.

If pickets enter the struck facility in pursuit of an individual, either to capture him or to inflict bodily harm on him, the security force must immediately rescue that individual and afford him sanctuary *while he is on company property.* The Security Operations Center should be notified of the situation and, in all probability, will notify local police.

Strikers must not be allowed to put any obstructions or barricades on company property. All such obstructions are illegal. If they block access gates or public traffic outside the perimeter, local police, not the company's security force, must correct the situation.

If a Security Officer is not positive that a person is authorized on company property during a strike, he should ask to see that individual's identification card or special pass and then then compare names and photographs with the individual concerned.

Should a striking employee or other unauthorized person be discovered on company property, the Security Officer should:

a. Apprehend and detain the individual. That means to stop him for questioning. Unless that individual has been seen committing an illegal act or unless he threatens or attempts to attack the Security Officer, he is not put under physical restraint. During pre-strike training periods, the Security Director must make certain that all Security Officers understand the meaning of "apprehend," "detain," "arrest." Security Officers have no powers of arrest. They shouldn't even use the word. If it seems appropriate, let the local police do it. This is a very sensitive legal area and improper action by a Security Officer can result in suits against the company.

b. Alert the nearest Observation and Documentation team to witness the apprehension and subsequent actions by the security staff. Alert the Security Operations Center.

c. Attempt to escort the intruder to the nearest security post and contact the Security Operations Center for further instructions.

d. If the intruder resists, he should be asked to leave the company property. Obviously, if he has been seen damaging property or performing some other illegal act, he should be detained until local police can be summoned. Force should never be used unless necessary to protect apprehending Security Officers or to prevent damage to company property. Under no circumstances should Security Officers lose sight of the individual until he leaves company property.

e. As soon as possible, all Security Officers and other witnesses (*e.g.,* Observation and Documentation team members) should complete Incident Reports covering the incident.

Security Officers' reports are very important. They will be covered in more detail in a subsequent chapter. Each Security Officer, proprietary or contract agency, must complete his own separate daily activity report. He should prepare it in chronological format, as events occur (*e.g.,* a patrol round, a telephone call, an incident) rather than wait until the end of his shift. He must submit that report before going off duty. Reports must be reviewed and initialed by his supervisor before that supervisor goes off duty. Incident Reports must be prepared as soon as possible after the incident occurs and must be cross-referenced to the Security Officer's activity report for that shift.

Security staff reports (Security Officers, investigators, Observation and Documentation teams, etc.), augmented by substantiating data or photographic evidence, are the most critical evidence needed to support company assertions in criminal prosecution cases or civil litigation arising from the strike.

During a labor dispute the individual Security Officer really earns his pay and has the opportunity to earn the respect and admiration of his fellow employees, his supervisors and local law enforcement agencies. How well he does his job largely determines how well the labor dispute can be confined to the facility itself and the overall tone, nature and duration of the strike.

CHAPTER 15

LAW ENFORCEMENT AGENCIES

Generally, the most critical time of a strike is at the beginning when massive picket lines block access to the struck facility. Labor and management leaders are uncertain about what is happening or about to happen. Both sides test the others' capabilities and resolve.

The first few days are especially important. The tone and direction of the strike have not yet been determined. The union's strategy may not yet be firmed. The number of pickets and their conduct is still unknown. There may be a lot of drinking at the scene. Strikers are excited, susceptible to peer pressure, bolstered by seeing the largest picketing force they may be able to muster during the strike. Sporadic and then increasing disorder may result—if not from the actions of individual picketers then from organized probes to determine how much the union can restrict company operations before local police intervene.

Union and management weigh the degree and quality of law enforcement at the scene. If they feel the police intend to remain neutral, impartially enforcing the law and maintaining order, there will be little trouble by either side. That's the way the strike will go. On the other hand, if police are slow to become involved or inept in enforcing law and order, one side or the other may attempt to exploit that weakness.

As the strike progresses, shift changes always will be critical times. So will shipments to or from the struck facility. Each succeeding Monday may be critical as the start of the week usually means maximum effort by the union to show its strength on the picket lines.

The second Monday may be more critical than the first. If the company paid striking employees as soon as the strike began, the second Monday will see no pay checks. For the first time strikers will feel the strike in their wallets. They're apt to be more militant, more demanding, less patient, more determined to force a resolution to their dispute.

Another critical period will come when some employees, deciding to return to work, cross picket lines for the first time. Sometimes this turns picket lines into skirmish lines.

During these times the Security Director may need all the police help he can get to prevent mass disorder, riot, damage to persons or property.

That help is going to be a lot more forthcoming and a lot quicker getting there if management, particularly the Security Director, understands the legal and practical side of law enforcement in such situations.

Legally, law enforcement agencies are required to preserve order and to protect property and citizens from harm. On the practical side, they don't like to get involved in what they may consider to be a private argument between a company and its employees. They also are very mindful of local politics. And their resources are limited.

It's important that managers understand this practical side of law enforcement, particularly in smaller communities. Most citizens obey the law. Local police resources, geared to handle a few individuals outside the law, may not be able to handle the massive numbers involved in an all-out donnybrook at the local stamping plant's main gate. Small communities may have only three or four police officers. They can't do much, particularly when a struck facility is only a small part of the community's general public safety problem.

The company seeks a court restraining order or permanent injunction. Injunctions take time: time to document, time to schedule a court hearing, time to present, time to wait for the judge's decision and implementing order. And, like their lesser municipal and county counterparts, judges are reluctant to restrain local voters unless it is absolutely necessary.

Thus the company may have the letter of the law on its side. Getting it enforced, however, may be another matter indeed. Management should realize this. Good relations between the company and local police officials are critical. They are not won overnight. They are a continuing, year-round public relations matter. Key to it all is the personality, technical competence and attitude of the Security Director. He must win the cooperation and support of his counterparts in public law enforcement. Even more, he must have that confidence and support to the extent that he can influence their decisions in a strike involving his facility.

The local Chief of Police or county Sheriff may never have handled a strike situation. He may want to do all he can to maintain or restore order but simply may not know how to do it. If there is mutual trust and confidence between him and the Security Director, that Security Director may be able to cause a number of police actions that will help the struck company.

As early as possible the Security Director should warn local police and the sheriff's office, verbally and in writing, of an impending strike. This was discussed earlier but the alert should include all the information available about when the strike is expected, the number of employees involved, the union involved, the number of pickets and type of problems anticipated, the company's intent to conduct business as usual or to restrict company operations—anything that may help local police weigh their responsibilities and the resources they'll need to meet those responsibilities.

The company also should notify local police of such things as the precise extent of the company's premises and the designation of access gates for employees, for contractors, for shipping and receiving.

The start of the strike should be immediately reported to local law enforcement agencies, verbally and in writing, with follow-up on more detailed information on exactly what is happening and the trouble anticipated.

The Security Operations Center should keep a record of all communications with law enforcement agencies and those agencies' responses. This record should show in as much detail as possible:

a. Who made the call? With whom did he talk?

b. What was said? What was decided? What commitments were made?

c. What has resulted from the call?

Written communications should be similarly recorded, with annotations for the record documenting results or follow-ups.

The Security Director should invite a local police representative to attend any pre-strike conference he may arrange between himself and the union's representatives. This meeting was discussed earlier but it bears repeating. Its purpose is to set a tone, a commitment for both sides to deal fairly and honestly with each other in upholding public order and maintaining the peace. It has nothing to do with strike issues or with negotiations to resolve them.

At the meeting the following ground rules might be adopted by labor, management, police:

a. Force or violence will not be tolerated.

b. The law will be enforced with strict impartiality.

c. The right of the public to use streets and sidewalks affected by the strike will be protected.

d. Unlawful conditions or acts which lead to disorder will not be tolerated.

e. Use of professional bullies or thugs will not be tolerated.

f. Use of professional agitators will not be tolerated.

g. No parties to the dispute may use language or other actions offensive to public decency or which may provoke violence.

h. The right of striking employees to picket in a peaceful and lawful manner will be protected.

i. Striking employees may picket the facility to persuade those still employed to join the strikers; to persuade those considering employment at the facility not to do so; to publicize the labor dispute. The number of pickets and the manner of their picketing, however, shall be limited to an agreement reached at this meeting.

j. Each representative at this union-management-police meeting will enforce this agreement among his followers.

k. Each representative at this union-management-police meeting will keep the other two representatives informed of developments affecting maintenance of public order and will meet, as required, to resolve issues which may threaten public order.

The Security Director should represent management at this meeting; the local police chief or his representative represent the local law enforcement agencies; the strike committee chairman or chief picket captain represent striking employees.

If that meeting can go well, and, if the principal parties to it can continue to work together in good faith, the chances of violence, mass disorder, damage to property or harm to individuals are greatly lessened and the seeds already sowed for restored good feeling after the dispute is resolved and employees return to work.

As a follow-up to this pre-strike meeting, local police might establish a temporary operational base near the struck facility. It should have telephone and radio tie-ins with the Security Operations Center and with the striking employees' strike headquarters.

The proximity of this temporary police operational base near the struck facility helps liaison between the police and the Security Director. If the union also can be represented there, all parties can meet on neutral ground, as often as necessary, to iron-out disputes concerning conduct of the pickets and like matters.

By these meetings the Security Director can insure that management's version of what might have occurred in a particular incident is heard by the police. Often that may provide information or actual facts or other documentation which strengthens the company's position.

This temporary police operational base also can provide food, shelter, bedding for police officers and a place for mobilizing and dispatching police reserves. It will keep some police officers near the struck facility all or part of the time. That can't help but have a good effect in maintaining order.

The role of police officers in enforcing open access to and from a struck facility already has been discussed. If they can do this, and generally maintain order, the Security Director is going to accomplish his mission in protecting his company and its employees during the dispute.

There are certain basic principles or operational procedures which police officers should follow in meeting their responsibilities during a labor dispute. The Security Director can't force them upon the local Chief of Police or Sheriff. But if he has established and maintained good working relationships with these individuals he should keep these ideas in mind and plant them where necessary and where possible:[6]

a. Police Conduct.

(1) Things to do.

(a) Be absolutely impartial and neutral. The job of the police department is to protect life, property, the rights of citizens; to direct and regulate traffic; to preserve order. Not to discuss strike issues, not to take sides. When an arrest is necessary, make it whether the offender is an employer or an employee.

(b) Get to know the disputants. Talk with them when you think it advantageous. But hold such conversations to a minimum and then primarily with the picket line captain and senior company official only.

(c) Charge the picket line captain or senior company official present with carrying out your instructions.

(d) Keep the general public away from the dispute.

(e) Be wary of professional agitators or any persons or any activities that may give the impression you have chosen sides.

(f) Keep your supervisors fully informed.

(g) Arrange for periodic reliefs for your men.

(2) Things not to do.

(a) Do not give the impression, by waving, smirks, gestures, words that you are biased in the dispute.

(b) Do not become provoked by name calling, gestures, other provocative acts directed at you.

(c) Do not go in numbers solely to get information at the scene of a confrontation. That makes people nervous. Show strength only when you intend to use it if necessary.

(d) Do not enter company property unless specifically summoned there for an emergency situation.

(e) Do not talk over the merits of the dispute.

(f) Do not discuss an injunction with anyone involved in the dispute.

(g) Do not accept gifts, even doughnuts and coffee. This gives the impression of partiality.

(h) Do not drink coffee or eat in restaurants frequented by disputants.

(i) Do not use toilet facilities, telephones, other conveniences on company property.

(j) Do not perform a police task immediately after conversing with a disputant. It gives the impression you are taking orders from him.

(k) Do not let a plant Security Officer assist the police on public property.

b. Picket Activity.

(1) Strikes and picketing, peacefully conducted, are lawful activities.

(2) A picket does not have to be an employee of the struck company.

(3) No specific number of pickets has been set (or as specified at the pre-strike meeting). Provided they picket peacefully and do not impede passage along sidewalks, streets, into or from the struck facility, they can have any number of pickets.

(4) Picket lines formed on sidewalks shall confine themselves to the outside or curb side so as not to passage.

(5) Pickets shall not form along or on streets or roads in such way as to impede traffic or constitute a safety hazard to others or to themselves.

(6) Pickets must keep moving with sufficient distance (about five feet) between them to permit passage of non-pickets without fear of physical contact.

(7) Pickets shall not intimidate individuals passing by or through their lines. Intimidation can be by physical threat, by presence, by spoken word.

(8) When a picket line stops or becomes unruly, it becomes a mob and subject to arrest. A mob consists of three (3) persons or more.

(9) Pickets may not block a door, driveway, or other entrance or exit to a struck plant or place of business.

(10) Pickets may not impede traffic, whether pedestrian, vehicle, or railroad.

(11) Anyone who wishes to go into or out of a place of business where there is a labor dispute, may do so without being impeded, stopped, or threatened with bodily harm. This also applies to movement of goods or other material.

(12) Union officials or pickets may talk to people going into or out of a struck facility. They may go to their homes to talk with them or may talk with them anywhere, provided they are orderly and do not intimidate, threaten or attempt to coerce. If a non-striker or non-picket does not want to talk with the union official or picket, he does not have to and must be allowed to go his way unimpeded and without being threatened, intimidated or coerced.

c. Disorderly Conduct.

(1) Fighting, assault, battery, violence, threats or intimidation will not be permitted.

(2) Firearms, knives, clubs and other weapons will not be permitted.

(3) Drinking.

(a) Police must be alert for drinking and drunkeness and should take immediate steps to restrict it. They should give special attention to local bars.

(b) Union officials should be alerted and given an opportunity to take proper action in the case of pickets' drinking alcoholic beverages or drunken pickets. If this does not work, police should arrest the individuals concerned.

(4) Sound trucks can be a serious disturbance. Caution operators to keep the volume down.

(5) Profanity and lewd language, gestures, or other similar conduct is contrary to public sensitivity and will not be tolerated.

(6) Where picket lines are disorderly, police officers should be stationed a short distance apart, facing the picketers.

(7) Individuals arrested for disorderly conduct should be processed as in non-strike situations.

d. Traffic.

(1) Police must remove any barriers, particularly barricades across streets, railroads, driveways, entrance ways and exits. If cars are blocking egress and drivers cannot be located, the vehicles must be towed away with the usual traffic charge.

(2) If egress to railroad trains or to trucks is blocked, police officers should stop the vehicle then move all pickets to the side. They should arrest anyone who insists on blocking egress. Then they should direct the engine (or truck) to enter or leave, cautioning the operator to proceed cautiously.

(3) Police should give verbal directions (rather than hand signals) when asked directions by a disputant. They should not lead them to a police vehicle or give hand signals as this may be interpreted as taking sides in the dispute or directing them to enter or leave a disputed area.

(4) A union official or picket may talk with truck drivers attempting to enter or leave a struck facility. The police officer should be present to insure that no threat, coercion or intimidation is involved. The police officer must not advise the operator whether to enter or not enter the struck facility. On the contrary, he should tell that individual that the choice is the operator's alone.

(5) The police department alone is charged with directing traffic. Outsiders should not be permitted to assist.

(6) Parades may be organized as a guise to avoid legal restrictions on picket lines. The police department is in sole control of traffic and the regulation and direction of traffic. Parades require permits. Mobs, consisting of three or more persons, are subject to arrest.

e. Police escort.

(1) It should not be necessary to give individuals protection away from the plant or business. Where serious threats are made, however, an officer may be stationed at the home of threatened persons.

(2) Police should not ride people from the plant or business in a police car except in an extreme emergency to protect them from bodily

injury. It is better to prevent the injury by keeping everyone orderly. Police are supposed to keep picket lines orderly and egress clear. Escorts through picket lines, therefore, should not be necessary.

(3) If pickets get into an automobile and follow a truck or car leaving the struck facility, a squad car should follow both. If the truck or car is not molested, the police should not interfere. If the following automobile attempts to cut the truck or car off, or to interfere with it in any other way that creates a traffic hazard, its occupants should be arrested.

(4) When some employees continue to work at a struck facility, the police should provide coverage a few minutes before starting and quitting times and remain on the scene until all have safely come and gone. A larger force is not necessary unless conduct of the picketers warrants it.

f. If Continued Arrests Have Failed to reduce the threat of serious trouble at a struck facility; if violence, serious threats and other disorders have occurred and probably will continue; and if the number of pickets makes enforcement difficult, if not impossible, the local police department should call for help of county or state police.

Employers should be seeking civil remedies but state police help in restoring order should not be delayed pending the outcome of the injunction request. When a request for relief is before the courts, the police department should anticipate that its officers will have to testify as to the conduct of the pickets and that photographs or other police material may be subpoenaed by the struck employer.

During a labor dispute, public law enforcement agencies, particularly local police, must deal with the mass movement and conduct of individuals who do not behave as they normally would. In such instances, the police department must maintain control of the situation and enforce the law fairly, strictly, impartially, and above all, quickly.

The existence of a strike does not license people to break laws or to threaten or disrupt public order. Nor does it license them to do as a group the things they are not permitted to do individually.

There are ample laws to keep labor disputes and the people involved in them peaceful and orderly. When those disputants, labor and management alike, know that those laws will be enforced, they will think before they violate them. Thus law and order can prevail during a labor dispute with minimum police involvement.

CHAPTER 16

SUPERVISORS' ORIENTATION

A sound leadership principle for any enterprise is that the leader should keep his subordinates informed. That is particularly true in a strike situation where supervisors are working in a difficult environment, possibly enduring picket line jibes of fellow employees twice a day and required to handle new and additional job responsibilities. If those supervisors feel that they are an important part of the company's management team and that they share company confidences, they will be better motivated. And, even if the light at the end of the strike tunnel is not yet visible, they'll feel more secure if at least they have some idea where they are.

There is danger, however, in sharing too much information about the strike. Some supervisors may not want or need to hear it. It may just put beans in their ears, something more to worry about. And it may leak information to striking employees—information on bargaining positions, the general state of company operations and security measures—information management would rather they didn't have.

Managers below the executive level often have mixed loyalties in a labor dispute. Many have come up from the ranks. They've been with the company for years, but they've also worked side-by-side with other employees for just as many years. Their personal loyalties may be to those friends. They may see the company as a large, impersonal organization. They are concerned about their own jobs, but they still can sympathize with striking employees.

They see no harm in sharing confidences with those striking employees. "Why Jack understands my position," rationalizes a shift supervisor. "He knows I've got to work. All supervisors have a job to do. That doesn't mean I'm against him. Why, I want to see them get all they can from this company. Heaven knows, the company can spare a few dollars. Besides, Jack's not one of those crazies. He's not going around putting sugar in gas tanks and stuff like that. If I gripe about how it's going in here he'll know I'm on his side. When this strike is over I've got to live with him and a heck of a lot more just like him. Live with all of them. And six more years 'til my pension."

Mixed loyalties and careless talk can cause unauthorized disclosure of company information. Sometimes that can do a lot of harm. So, although it's a good idea to keep subordinates informed, the principle has to be tempered with another: Are they *authorized* to receive this information and do they *need* to know it to do their jobs?

Depending on the group being oriented, the briefer should present a general orientation with specifics only as authorized within that group and as they need the information to do their jobs.

As part of management's pre-strike activities, supervisors should be given a general orientation on the strike situation. Once the strike begins and details become more definite, a second oral briefing may follow. During the strike, company executives periodically should meet with their managers, the managers with their supervisors and supervisors with non-striking employees to keep individuals generally informed of the labor dispute and of company operations. Written bulletins or memoranda also can be posted for employee reading to disseminate general information.

Management also can communicate with both striking and non-striking employees by personal letters. Remember, however, that in communications between management and labor there are pitfalls. The National Labor Relations Board will permit an employer to communicate directly with employees through non-coercive communications that present:

a. Information on the status of negotiations.

b. Explanations of positions the employer previously offered the union at the bargaining table or stated in depositions of grievances.

c. Refutations of inflammatory charges openly made by the union.

d. Criticism of bargaining strategy and related union leadership tactics which management insists cause the strike to continue.

The danger to management's direct approach to employees, however, is that if it is coupled with a *fixed position* by management at the bargaining table, the NLRB may see the letter as an unlawful attempt to bypass and undermine the union as the employees' bargaining agent. That would be an unfair labor practice.

With that restriction in mind, however, management should try to keep all employees current on the status of negotiations and affirm the idea that the company would like for everyone to return to work.

Supervisors' oral briefings can be made by a management team, with representatives from the executive management, personnel, operations, legal and security areas. They include the following matters.

The Personnel Director or Industrial Relations Manager might orient supervisors on the basis for the strike. What are the issues involved? He should state the union's demands and the company's response. He should describe the progress of negotiations and the latest bargaining position of both sides. He may give some indication of where he expects the bargaining process to go from there and its prospects of an early settlement. Then, in conjunction with other staff representatives, such as finance, production, operations, he may wish to discuss, in general terms, financial problems or concerns the strike is causing the company. Supervisors should be briefed on strike-related changes to company operations. Will the company attempt to continue "business as usual" or will some activities be limited during the strike. Which ones? Which areas will be closed? Which ones activated? Will some operations be consolidated? Will raw materials and supplies be received during the strike? Will finished goods be stock-piled or shipped from the facility?

Included might be a discussion of whether all or some employees will remain on-site during the strike. Which employees? Which departments? What arrangements have been made for their logistical support: quarters, food, personal comforts, recreation? Will shifts be changed? Will car pools be organized? Will alternate means of transportation be provided by the company? What are they and how will they work?

The legal staff should follow with a discussion of pertinent aspects of federal, state and local labor laws. The briefings shouldn't attempt to make anyone an expert on the National Labor Relations Act or the Taft-Hartley Act but, if those or other acts have specific application to the strike in question, it may be well to indicate that application with specific examples that bring it down to a working level.

The legal staff's orientation should include prohibited strike activities. What are secondary boycotts and how might they apply here? What is meant by mass picketing and what are its characteristics? Is it likely to be seen in this strike? What is meant by "violence," "intimidation," "threats," "coercion"? How might they be practiced in this strike? What will be the company policy regarding those arrested for criminal offenses or for destruction of company property?

Earlier, in discussing Observation and Documentation teams, we considered a number of possible strikers' actions that are illegal. These should be reviewed with supervisors as specific examples of what could happen and what they should be alert for and report to the security staff.

The supervisors' orientation might include information on company policy on standing behind repair or replacement of employees' property damaged as a direct result of strikers' actions. Supervisors have a right to know these things before they risk their own property or urge non-striking workers to do the same in crossing picket lines. They also need to be reminded to report these incidents without delay.

Supervisors should be aware of the company's legal defenses against improper strike activities. These defenses might include legal restraints, permanent injunctions, civil suits, criminal actions, disciplinary action against employees involved. The company should state its intent to pursue any and all of these remedies and, if some already have begun, their status.

This portion of the legal briefing should include instructions on legal requirements for the company to prove its case in any of these legal actions. They should know that Observation and Documentation teams will document improper activities and that the security staff will investigate all reported violence, coercion, threat or intimidation, injury to individuals, or damage to company or employee property during the strike. Supervisors will be charged with noting any striker misconduct and immediately reporting it to the Security Operations Center or the nearest Observation and Documentation team. They also may be asked to provide affidavits or other statements concerning incidents they have witnessed.

Throughout the supervisors' orientations management should make clear its support of the Security Department and point out that its security measures work to the benefit of everyone concerned in the dispute.

Management also should make clear its intent to discipline or discharge employees engaged in misconduct and that, although an individual's right to strike in legal manner is protected, once that individual involves himself in improper strike activities he can be disciplined or fired. If any briefing information is going to leak to striking employees, this would be an excellent bit to have passed along.

Supervisors' orientations must include a code of conduct to govern non-striking employees proceeding to or from work, singly, in car pools, in company-provided transportation. It also should include guidance on any strike-related incidents at their homes or otherwise away from the facility itself. Most important, it must include guidance on crossing picket lines.

Let's review picket line guidance. During strikes picketers tend to crowd personnel and vehicles attempting to enter or leave company premises. This causes unnecessary but very real safety hazards. An individual crossing picket lines should observe the following precautions:

a. As much as possible, car pool or use company-furnished transportation, even if only for the last few miles.

b. Park private vehicles only in designated areas inside the facility. If individuals plan to form car pools somewhere outside the facility, their rallying point should be far enough away to avoid strikers' observation and possible confrontation. If vehicles are to be left unattended, the meeting point should be a heavily traveled site.

c. Individuals should plan to stay inside the facility for their entire shift. Emergency trips across picket lines should be coordinated with the Security Operations Center.

d. Proceed through picket lines with great care at all times. If police officers are on duty, follow their directions. They may not give hand signals and cannot advise individuals to enter or not to enter the struck facility. That decision is an individual one.

e. Remember that employees have the legal right to free access to and from company work areas at all times. The worker must gradually work his vehicle through the picket line. He must not run into anyone; must not run into any obstruction; must not use force; must not cause a confrontation.

f. He must ignore any verbal abuse from the pickets. He must concentrate on the proper and safe operation of his vehicle, keeping car windows closed and not exchanging words or gestures with pickets. Any comments or gestures by non-strikers, no matter how well intentioned, may be taken wrong and cause a confrontation. Any comments or gestures by strikers, no matter how personal or vulgar, must be ignored. Failure to do that would only worsen the situation. Drivers must remain calm, cool, patient.

g. If pickets refuse to allow a car to pass, the driver should sound its horn and proceed slowly until he has room to pass through the picket line. The horn also will notify police that he needs help. If the pickets still refuse to let a driver pass, he should not force the issue. He should retreat to a safe distance and call the Security Operations Center for guidance. In these instances, he should remember the names and faces, all he saw and heard, and make notes on them for reporting to the security staff.

    h. If nails or other obstacles are thrown over the roadway, the driver should not drive over them. He should report them to local police and the company security staff. The driveway will be swept.

If non-striking employees are followed by picketers, they should avoid confrontation or taking any act which could aggravate the situation. If the following picketers do not attempt to interfere with the safe operation of the vehicle or otherwise threaten or actually harm the non-striking employee or his vehicle, they should be ignored. If they do cause risk or actual damage to property, or to himself or to others, the non-striking employee still should take no action that would provoke a fight or other serious incident. As quickly as possible, however, he should report the incident to local police and to the security staff.

Escorts should not be necessary. If they are, it means that local police are not doing their job of maintaining order and assuring free access to company premises. These instances are grounds for court-ordered sanctions on the union and its striking employees.

Any strike-related damage to an employee's home or other personal property, or any threats of harm to that personal property or to the employee or his family, should be reported immediately to local police and to the Security Operations Center.

The major portion of supervisors' pre-strike or strike orientations probably will be conducted by the Security Director. It will include a variety of topics. While he is attempting to win their support to his security program, however, he should always keep in mind the danger of unauthorized disclosure of sensitive information.

Supervisors must know the company chain-of-command during a strike emergency. Who is responsible for what operations? How can that individual be contacted in emergencies? What authority has been delegated to him?

Supervisors also must know the physical limits of company property and that security within that boundary is the responsibility of the security department; outside that boundary is the responsibility of local law enforcement agencies.

Supervisors must know any changes to normal communications procedures. They should have emergency phone numbers related to their own areas of responsibility. They should be given numbers of appropriate additional phones that may be established for the emergency. If any supervisors not normally involved in radio communications will be using radios during the strike, they need a thorough indoctrination and practice in the use of that equipment. All supervisors should be reminded of the need for telephone and radio security. Communications can be monitored. Supervisors must be constantly wary of unintentionally divulging company information to eavesdroppers.

Supervisors must understand the mission, the responsibilities and authority of the security guard force. The presence of additional contract guards, their uniforms and other means of identification, their supervision by the proprietary guard staff, their particular assignments—should be reviewed. Supervisors should report to the Security Operations Center any improprieties or improper attitudes by Security Officers.

Personnel identification systems probably will change during the strike. Supervisors must be briefed on emergency personnel identification badges, their issuance and use, their accountability when the strike ends. They must know changes to shift schedules and to time card or time clock procedures. They must know of any changes to package and material control procedures or for inspection of packages or other material being taken from the facility.

Throughout the supervisors' orientations, briefers should emphasize that the tightening of security measures is necessary to protect the company and to protect individuals from harm.

The security briefer will outline use of access gates. Which gates are for personnel use? Which for vehicular traffic? Which for contractors? He must make clear that these gates are to be used only for the purpose designated and that no other gates or means of access are to be used.

During the strike, the security force will be particularly vigilant to detect and apprehend trespassers. If non-striking employees remain on-site during the strike, before long some of them are going to attempt to leave the facility. It's time to go home, they'll reason, whether the company likes it or not. A good security staff will know the methods and routes these individuals will attempt to use. In supervisor orientations the security representative should make it clear that leaving the facility without permission or by unauthorized measures can result in non-striking workers' injury by besieging strikers who will be watching from outside the perimeter.

Supervisors must be challenged to report all unidentified or unknown individuals they see on company property. This is true at all times, but particularly during a strike. Employees, vendors, visitors must wear identification badges on their outer garments so long as they are on company property. Visitors must be escorted at all times when on company property. Violators should be challenged by supervisors and, if appropriate, reported to the nearest Observation and Documentation team or Security Officer.

Pertinent supervisors must be alerted to any changes in shipping and receiving procedures; the necessity of coordinating beforehand with the Security Operations Center the use of marshalling points outside the facility to schedule picket line crossings in shipping and receiving; absolute requirements that drivers be properly licensed and qualified; tightened identification procedures for commercial carriers; tightened vehicle safety and security inspections by the security staff.

Non-striking employees must be alerted to any changes to traffic patterns within the facility during the strike and of designated parking areas. Supervisors must help enforce those measures and see that employees park only in assigned areas.

Supervisors must know of general changes to patrol plans or other measures by which the security staff will protect the facility. This includes additional or changed coverage. Supervisors, more familiar with work areas, may note gaps in that coverage. If so, they should immediately report it.

If supervisors are to complete any security reports, as for individuals assigned picket line testing or those designated for Observation and Documentation teams, they should be well oriented in those responsibilities. Report writing will be discussed in detail a bit later in this text.

Supervisors and their subordinates must know that anyone can submit an Incident Report to the Security Operations Center. This would be a self-initiated (as opposed, for example, to a witness interview) report of any security or safety hazard or of improper action that that individual thinks should be called to the attention of the security staff. The security briefer should emphasize that all Incident Reports, verbal or written, will be investigated by a security staff member. This is to encourage employee input to the security program by letting individuals know that their contributions count.

A final matter that should be covered in supervisors' orientations, and this probably will be done by the legal or personnel representative, is the matter of supervisors' oral communications with employees. What information about the strike can a supervisor discuss with his subordinates?

During a strike, supervisors frequently talk with the people who work for them. Whatever discussions take place, the supervisors must conduct themselves and present information consistent with the company's strike communication program. By this I mean that they follow guidance suggested earlier in this text about communications between management and labor during a strike. Supervisors can discuss current negotiations so long as they confine themselves to matters already openly brought to the bargaining table or stated in legal grievance procedures; to matters that refute highly inflammable and incorrect union charges; to current offerings by the company so long as those "current offerings" are not known to be fixed, unalterable positions. The supervisor may criticize a union tactic if he feels that tactic makes impossible a solution fair and reasonable to both sides, but he *cannot* seem to defame or undermine the union, *per se*, before the employees.

More specifically, if approached by an employee, the supervisor could:

a. Tell the employee that the law permits the company to hire a permanent replacement for anyone who engages in an economic strike.

b. Remind the employee of the benefits the employee presently enjoys. He must avoid, however, veiled threats or promises about future benefits.

c. Tell the employee that false promises or statements by outsiders should be disregarded and that the company has no knowledge of those matters. If there is no threat of the company's closing, he may assure the employee that the company's desire is only to keep the facility as busy as possible.

d. Point out the disadvantages which result from a strike, such as loss of income, being required to serve on a picket line, loss of benefits.

e. State that during negotiations the company, he feels, has believed its proposals to be fair, in good faith, in everyone's best interest.

f. Urge employees to consider what is in their own best interest, now and for the future.

g. Urge the employee not to threaten, insult or ridicule employees on strike. They'll all have to live together after the strike.

h. Warn the employee not to spy on any other employees or to engage in any arguments with them.

i. Urge the employee not to make any statements about the strike to the news media. Let the negotiators handle it.

Everyone likes to feel that he matters to the company which employs him. Matters a lot. In a strange and stressful environment, like a strike, everyone also likes to have some idea of what is going on and the prospects for an end to that stressful situation. Management needs all the help it can get from its supervisors, particularly during a labor dispute. Keeping those supervisors informed of as much as they safely can and should know of strike-related matters is a worthwhile management technique.

CHAPTER 17

RECORDS AND REPORTS

Every event relating to the strike, regardless of its seeming insignificance at the time, should be reported to the Security Operations Center and be recorded for analysis and possible use in planning strike management strategy or in seeking injunctive reliefs, in criminal prosecutions, in civil suits, in personnel actions.

Individuals who normally would be expected to submit periodic reports (Security Officers, supervisors, members of Observation and Documentation teams) should be instructed in basic report writing and in the specifics of the type report they are most likely to use. If time does not permit this orientation before the strike, it should be given as soon as possible after the strike begins, if only in the form of constructive critiques of reports as they are submitted. It will do little good if an individual observes something of significance to the strike situation but is unable to accurately tell his supervisor about it.

It also is important that report writers receive some feedback on their input. Is the report complete, accurate, concise? Can it be understood correctly? Does it say what the writer wants it to say? Does it cover the who, what, when, where, why (as appropriate) of the incident? Does it label hearsay information? Is it properly supported by documentation, when appropriate? Are individuals and incidents cited in the report identified as completely and as accurately as possible? As early as possible, the report writer should be critiqued on his observation techniques and on his report writing skill. If he has not done well, he should be shown how he can improve his work. If he has done well, he's earned a pat on the back.

Regardless of the quality of the report writer's work, he must know that someone has read, understood, considered his effort.

The Security Operations Center should be adequately stocked with all necessary logs and other report forms. Copy equipment should be easily accessible for additional copies.

Operational Summary

The Security Director should prepare a daily operational summary to provide management with an up-to-date summary of all events occurring during the previous twenty four-hour period. It should reference individual Security Officer reports, Incident Reports, photographs, statements of witnesses, affidavits, audio tapes, movies, Observation and Documentation team logs or other documentary evidence for greater detail.

The daily operational summary also should contain descriptive information on strike activities:

a. Time the picket line was established, discontinued, resumed, changed in composition or tactics, as appropriate.

b. The number of pickets, picket leaders, picket equipment seen or used.

c. Areas operating and areas closed in struck facility.

d. Picket conduct, mood, morale, equipment.

e. Police strength and activity.

f. Picket observers: numbers, locations, activity, attitude toward strikers or toward company.

g. Presence of union leaders, local and national, and their activity.

h. Presence of weapons, signs, drinking.

i. Management activities: picket line testing, shipping and receiving, discussion with striking union on local tactical situation, agreements; liaison with law enforcement agencies or government labor agencies; future scheduled activities.

j. Number of employees crossing picket lines during reported period; summary of problems they encountered.

k. Summary of all Incident Reports, documentary evidence obtained that day.

l. Miscellaneous information regarding the strike.

Violence or other unusual incidents should be detailed (and substantiated) more fully by appropriate documentation. When picketing is peaceful and in compliance with pre-strike agreements or injunctive proscriptions, it should be noted in the daily operational summary. Reporting both sides of the coin adds credibility to all reports.

Security Officer's Daily Activity Report

Each Security Officer must complete and submit a Security Officer's Daily Activity Report for each shift he works. It should contain the following information:

  a. Name.

  b. Date.

  c. Post location.

  d. Supervisor.

  e. Security Officer relieved and time of relief.

  f. Relieving Security Officer and time of relief.

  g. Receipt of equipment, logs, etc.

  h. Any noted fire, safety, security hazards.

  i. Chronological account of Security Officer's location and activity during the entire shift.

  j. Summary of any unusual activity, incidents witnessed by that Security Officer or reported to him. Entries should be cross-referenced to the appropriate Incident Report more fully describing the reported incident and to documentation of it. All individuals involved in the incident or having knowledge of it should be fully identified in the report. Some weeks from now the incident may assume considerable significance. Unless he has recorded details in this report (and on Incident Report), the Security Officer may not be able to recall them. His report cannot be too detailed.

Completed daily activity reports must be reviewed by the Security Officer's immediate supervisor before the shift ends. Delay may cause loss of specific information valuable to the Security Director.

Senior Security Officer's Report

This report is similar in format and intent to those of the individual Security Officer. The scope, however, is broader. This is a supervisor's report. He should record all assigned Security Officers and their assigned posts. He should report any problems pertaining to that shift (personnel late or absent, accidents or sickness on the job, equipment malfunctions, etc.). The Security Director should read these supervisors' reports. Every shift, every day. It is the way Security Officers communicate directly with him.

The Senior Security Officer must account for his supervisory activity during the shift (*e.g.,* "0400–0450: Inspected gate house; 0610–0645: Walked clock tour with S/O Jones") and for any absences from his post. He must reference Incident Reports received during his shift and, if appropriate, conduct follow-up investigations elaborating on the basic Incident Reports.

The Senior Security Officer should review reports of all personnel assigned him, critiquing their observation and report writing techniques, praising good work and correcting poor effort. He also must assure that outgoing Security Officers, in addition to completing their own reports, brief their replacements.

Senior Security Officers responsible for each group of Security Officers and special teams are critical to the company's strike management program. They make on-the-spot decisions regarding the security staffs' handling of picket line incidents and direct proper documenting of those incidents as they occur.

Incident Reports

All incidents of an unusual or questionably improper nature must be reported to the Security Operations Center. That can be done by anyone, whether he is a member of the security staff or not, who witnesses the incident or to whom it is reported. The Security Officer receiving a verbal report of such an incident should have the individual prepare an Incident Report to get the information first-hand. The Security Officer then can elaborate on it, as necessary, with his own report. Hearsay (second-hand) information, rumors or opinions must be clearly labeled as such.

All reports of violence should be investigated and traced back to their source. Examples might be threatening phone calls, damage to company property or that of individual employees, other acts of intimidation. Investigations may be by a team of security staff members specifically trained to conduct investigations. If the incident is more involved, as in the use of dynamite bombs, arson, or other sabotage of company facilities, it may be necessary to use professional investigators or for the Security Director to do it himself, in conjunction with appropriate civil authorities.

The important thing is for the Security Director to be informed of incidents as soon after they occur as possible. If the Security Director can prove that an illegal or otherwise improper action was committed by a striking employee or union member, it could deter future violence. If individuals who otherwise might be tempted to commit unlawful acts know that the Security Director will use all his resources to investigate those acts and identify perpetrators, they'll not be as apt to try them.

Incident Reports lead to these investigative efforts. They are very important. Individuals should be encouraged to use them to report anything they believe worth bringing to the attention of the Security Director.

Strike Logs

Strike logs document all activities noted during a strike situation. They are prepared by the Security Operations Center staff and by Observation and Documentation teams. The Security Operations Center staff also is responsible for preparing the Security Department's master strike log, a compilation of entries from the individual, separate logs.

Strike logs should indicate the date, time, location of the preparing groups, group members, summarize incidents and cross-reference appropriate Incident Reports containing more detailed information about those incidents, identify the individual preparing log entries.

Entries must be brief, clear, simple, legible, accurate. They should state facts or clearly label any hearsay information.

Strike logs should be opened as a team begins its duty shift, entered as events occur or are reported, completed with submission to the Security Operations Center at the end of the shift.

Strike Photography Log

These logs are kept by individuals of Observation and Documentation teams responsible for photographing incidents during a strike situation. They must clearly identify team members involved and the date, time, location of the team during that shift.

The Strike Photography Log should be cross-referenced with Incident Reports or other reports citing in more detail the incident photographed. Technical data on frame, type film, ASA number, etc., must be entered as it is important in any subsequent litigation to establish the credibility of the photographs involved.

The photographer should be clearly identified and he must make notes for future reference as soon as possible after an event occurs. These notes, or his formal reports, might be cross-referenced on the backs of the photographs concerned. Again, to give additional credibility to the photographer's work in documenting an incident.

Strike Video/Audio Tape Logs

These logs, similar in format to the Strike Photography Log, are used to record video or audio tape documentation taken during the strike. They too must cite dates and times and identify Observation and Documentation team members. They also should provide technical information such as tape numbers or counter start/stop numbers, specifically relating this portion of the video or audio tape to the incident described. The incident itself should be briefly identified in the log with reference to its more detailed Incident Report. The photographer or recorder responsible for each entry in the log also should be identified for future reference.

On the actual tapes of video or audio recordings, the photographer or recorder should introduce the taping with a few words identifying himself, stating the date and time, location, describing the incident about to be recorded or as it has been recorded on video/audio tape.

Strike Video/Audio Tape Logs should be opened as the shift begins, entered as events are recorded, completed when the team submits them to the Security Operations Center at the end of the shift.

Notes relating to incidents described in the log should be retained by team members for future reference if needed for testifying or further describing taped incidents.

Strike Trucking Log

The Strike Trucking Log is used to identify and document all company or commercial vehicles entering or leaving the struck facility. Dates, times, locations, the vehicle, its driver, his company, his cargo must be completely identified. Dates and times are important, particularly if an incident involving that vehicle occurs and the Strike Trucking Log is cross-referenced to an Incident Report about the incident.

Strike Trucking Logs should contain specific instructions for drivers, such as the following:

"Drivers must read and comply with the following:

a. Drivers must complete the above information.

b. Drivers must have a proper license, as required by the state, and insurance coverage.

c. Drivers must drive at a careful, safe, slow speed when crossing picket lines; use directional signals; comply with instructions of police or plant security force.

d. Drivers must keep windows closed, doors locked; must not talk to or make gestures to pickets; *must remain in vehicle's cab at all times.*

e. Drivers must follow company traffic manager's instructions as per route to enter or leave the plant.

Drivers must read these instructions and certify their understanding and willingness to comply with them by signing the form (witnessed by the Security Officer taking the data) before the driver is allowed to move the vehicle from the security check point.

Strike Trucking Logs must be completed before the shift ends for submission to the Security Operations Center.

Receiving Log

This log is used to register letters or packages received at the struck facility through the security staff. It must identify the dates, times and locations the material was received and times turned over to addressees. It also must identify senders and their addresses. Finally, the person to whom the Security Officer turns over the material must certify receipt of it by initialing the log.

Completed Receiving Logs should be certified by the Security Officer responsible for them and turned in to the Security Operations Center at the end of each shift.

Visitors Log

Visitors logs are an important tool, particularly during a strike situation, to document visitors to the struck facility. They must fully identify dates, locations, times, visitors' names and companies, persons or departments visited and the Security Officer or receptionist responsible for the log.

The Security Officer or receptionist should verify entries as soon as they are made and before allowing the individual to leave the security desk. This deters fraudulent or otherwise incomplete or improper entries. If escorts are assigned for visitors, their names should be noted in the visitors log. The Security Officer or receptionist should require all visitors to sign-out at the end of their visits.

Completed visitors logs should be certified by the individual responsible for entries on them and turned in to the Security Operations Center at the end of each shift.

It may appear that the various reports, logs and other forms recommended here are time-consuming and not worth the effort they involve. That is not true. The effort involved in maintaining *all* logs, reports and other forms is paid in full by a single successful investigation or litigation. Once an individual becomes accustomed to them, he can complete entries with little difficulty in little time. It becomes second nature. He does not mind doing it. Besides, during a strike there always is ample time when the security staff member simply is waiting. That is a good time to be sure that his reports are up-to-date.

Accurate, complete, neat, professional reports and logs are extremely important in supporting investigations and subsequent legal actions. These attributes lend credibility to the reports and logs and to the testimony of the individuals who prepared them. Days, weeks, months after an event occurred, those individuals may be required to testify about entries contained in their reports. Then it is perfectly appropriate for them to refer to these documents or to their notebooks during their court testimony.

The Security Director must insure that the work of his staff is thoroughly and professionally documented. Otherwise, much of their work may be of limited value.

CHAPTER 18

PICKET LINES

Although there can be strikes without picket lines and picket lines without strikes, the two generally are considered part and parcel of labor disputes. Picket lines may be the first indication that an industrial plant, a store or a truck center is involved in a labor dispute.

Picketing is difficult to define because its purpose and the way it is carried out vary. In its most acceptable form the picket line consists of one or two individuals walking back and forth in front of a store, office or plant, carrying placards proclaiming labor's concern with that employer. Such a picket line is designed to be informative, persuasive, urging workers and the general community to support the union's concerns.

Unions, however, do not always have the sympathy and support of the general public or even of a majority of the workers. In these cases they may try a far more aggressive form of picketing to force an early victory. Pickets' militancy also intensifies if the company attempts to operate the struck facility. Picketing becomes a major tactical weapon, a form of blockade, as strikers attempt to isolate the facility by stopping shipments and personnel from entering or leaving.

When someone attempts to cross the picket line, and especially if anyone challenges that picket line, the basic issues of the dispute become secondary. To the strikers their picket line is symbolic of their solidarity and determination. Attacking it is attacking them, personally and as a group. To show that solidarity and determination, they'll fight to maintain their picket line and to accomplish its purpose. *That* becomes the paramount issue, not economic issues under consideration, and it is more worth violent confrontation than "benefits" haggling.

The kind and intensity of picket activity varies widely depending upon such factors as the following:

a. The degree of workers' support for the strike. If the strike issue truly is a popular one with many workers involved, those workers will be more apt to fight for it. The picket line offers the best chance to demonstrate that determination.

b. The degree of workers' emotional involvement in the basic issues of the strike. A strike for wage benefits might have enduring support but be low-keyed. One for perceived unfairness, as in the questionable firing of a fellow employee, is far more emotional, far more apt to cause violence on the picket line.

c. The size and composition of the work force. Clerks and secretarial personnel normally are not going to be as militant or as willing to use force as might be steel workers, miners, truckers, particularly when there are large numbers involved and individuals see it as a way to let off steam against a variety of perceived abuses, symbolized by management, while finding some anonymity within a large group.

d. The attitude of the community as a whole toward the company, toward the union, toward strikes. If the community has witnessed a long history of violent labor confrontations, current picketing strikers are apt to remember that past and try to go it one better.

e. The employer's attitude toward the strike and toward the strikers. If his attitude is belligerent or demeaning, strike leaders will play that attitude to their advantage, rallying employees to strike back at it. If the employer attempts to continue "business as usual," he is sure to provoke strong resentment and firmer opposition by the picketing workers.

f. The militancy of the union involved. Certain unions, such as those representing truckers, construction workers, stevadores are known for the violence of their strikes.

g. The historical relationship between the company and its employees. If there has been a long history of strikes and retaliatory actions, there probably will be dangerous confrontations in current strikes.

h. Economic pressures upon labor and management. The company needs to bring raw materials and supplies across picket lines to continue to function; the workers, particularly in a long strike, begin to feel the economic pinch of check-less Mondays. Both sides may try to force a conclusion to the strike, a conclusion favorable to their side.

i. Picket line incidents that provoke violence or strengthen pickets' resolve. Strike tactics that seem to succeed may trigger violent reactions by the other side. Attempts by company officials to resupply the plant, angry words or obscene gestures by one side or the other, an impatient manager's horn honking or threat to run-over a picket often are enough to turn otherwise fairly well behaved individuals into a mob.[7]

To be alert to these and other factors which may influence the peacefulness of a picket line, the Security Director should understand something of the psychological factors operating upon striking employees, and something of the leadership problems facing union leaders during a strike.

At first, during most strikes, there will be tentative, uncertain activities by both sides. An attempt to establish positions, procedures; a calculated or unintentional probing to test reactions.

Strikers previously uninvolved in strikes, particularly in strikes involving picket line operations, may be hesitant and uncertain of what they are supposed to do. They'll have the basic idea that somehow the picket line is very important to their cause. They'll not know exactly *why* it is, but they'll feel it's very important for the picket line to do its job, whatever that job may be. They'll also have the idea that it's important to keep "scabs" from crossing that line, important that they keep the struck facility under siege. They'll not know how far they can go to accomplish those ends.

If the strike is hastily arranged, it will take a day or so to get the picket lines fully operational. Strike leaders must organize pickets into teams and shifts with assigned access gates to cover. They'll have to appoint picket line captains, prepare and issue signs, consider news releases. A strike headquarters will be necessary to coordinate activities. Often the union will establish a field kitchen near the strike scene to support pickets and perhaps all striking employees. It probably will be manned by "fence sitters," employees (union and non-union) who do not oppose the strike but don't want to serve on picket lines.

Union leaders also will need to establish union benefits, usually limited to those willing to devote some hours each day to picket line service. They also will arrange bail bond service for strikers arrested on strike duty.

Often the union leaders will push their own personal picket line activity to the far edge of legality. They'll want to be arrested. That will set an example and will put them in martyrs' roles. As far as the police are concerned, if arrests are necessary, Fridays are a good time to do it. It may be difficult over a weekend to arrange a hearing and proper bail so an especially belligerent leader can be kept out of harm's way for a bit longer.

The first confrontations may well set the tone for the entire strike. If pickets are pushed too hard, by management or police, they'll push back. The first supervisors or workers attempting to cross picket lines will meet as much resistance as pickets feel they can legally offer. The same applies to pickets' resistance to local police. If the strikers feel their right and ability to blockade the struck facility are threatened, pickets will be more prone to use *whatever* force is necessary to preserve their lines and *whatever* tactics they can get away with, legal or not.

Surprisingly, female strikers are apt to push back harder and quicker than men. Women known to be meek, quiet, unassertive on their jobs may become especially belligerent and aggressive on the picket line.

Early on there will develop a camaraderie among picketing strikers. They share a common strike goal. More important, as the strike develops, they'll draw closer among themselves as they realize that unity is their best weapon against a common "enemy,"—management.

Workers, who seldom if ever speak to each other on the job, will find that on the picket line they have plenty of time and interest in conversation with their co-workers. As the strike progresses, the picket line and other union-sponsored rallies will become a form of social gatherings. This is particularly true in rural or small town environments. Strikers will come to picket line duties as much for socializing with fellow workers as for the labor issues involved.

The socializing will extend to strike-related high jinks. A picket will appear costumed as a management figure central to the strike. Soon other strikers will assume roles of other management figures. They'll improvise skits and songs satirizing management, particularly company activities directed against the pickets but which failed.

Pickets may sing popular songs or parodies of popular songs improvised to fit their local situation. To the World War I favorite, "Mademoiselle from Armentieres":

> "Sam Brown's [company owner] become a nervous wreck, parlez vouz
> Sam Brown's become a nervous wreck, parlez vouz
> Sam Brown's become a nervous wreck,
> He'd surely like to break our necks
> Hinky, dinkey parlez vouz.

Or, to the tune of "Pistol-Packing Mama—Lay That Pistol Down":

> "Oh, take those scabs away, Tom
> Take those scabs away.
> Sign that union contract
> And we'll be back today.

Pickets will improvise humorous signs, costumes, games. Some of the high jinks can create real operational problems for the struck company:

noisemakers (air horns, sirens, bells, gongs, hammered sheet metal) to distract workers; large mirrors to direct bright, bothersome shafts of sunlight into office or manufacturing areas; oil, tar, automobile tires burned near loading docks so that, when doors are opened, the acrid fumes and smoke will be drawn into shipping and receiving work areas.

Management will counterattack with its own tactics. They may try to smuggle finished goods from the plant in supervisors' automobiles or, if the facility is closely barricaded and crossing picket lines is especially difficult, management may try to move supplies or goods into the facility by mail, parcel post or similar services. Once detected, these ploys are sure to be resisted.

In a long strike, so long as there is hope of winning, picketers will be bound by the group urge to "stick together." Bound more by that intangible instinct than by the basic issues in the dispute. Issues become blurred. The instinct to go on resisting for the "good of the group" becomes paramount. So long as some workers fight to maintain their picket lines, and so long as there is any chance of winning the strike, workers are more apt to continue the strike because of group loyalty than for the strike issues themselves.

Community groups may become involved, particularly in picket line activity, and particularly in small towns. Picket line action provides interest, amusement and vicarious thrills for passersby. The Security Director should be alert to the crowd's reaction to pickets' activities and, where possible, take advantage of that reaction.

Citizens' groups may form and take actions on their own to end the strike. The Security Director must watch for signs of support or antipathy toward the strike. He also must be alert for public safety dangers to large crowds of spectators.

Female picketers will be of particular interest to observers. The presence of female strikers and their activity, often more militant than the mens', can have considerable influence on the community's support of the strikers' cause.

One thing is sure. The strike is bound to be a chief topic of conversation within the community and strikers walking picket lines the focus of attention.

The Security Director must watch for any deviations from any pre-strike agreements: numbers of picketers, manner of picketing, use of profane or abusive language or gestures, threats to anyone attempting to cross picket lines. These deviations, caught early enough, might be nipped in the bud. Allowing them to continue, however, can only lead to worse tactics.

When drivers try to cross picket lines they should remain inside their vehicles, with windows closed. They should move cautiously, slowly but steadily while ignoring any taunts, jibes, threats or insults by picketers. Any response from them is likely to lead to violence. The security staff must be alert to notify police if trouble occurs outside the facility's perimeter and to document illegal acts, identifying troublemakers from either side in the dispute.

Strikers will try to discourage anyone's entering or leaving the facility. They may do this by walking closely together, by moving very slowly, or by not moving at all so as to block access. They will call out to drivers or approach accessing vehicles as closely as possible, then attempting to persuade or force the driver to turn around.

They may abandon a motor vehicle, stall its engine, or feign engine trouble to block the street or facility access. They may let air out of a vehicle's tires to cause moving it to be more difficult. The car may be driven to an entrance gate, then stalled. Other vehicles behind it can't move either and access is barred. The company should have a towing vehicle ready in these instances and film the scene to prove the public safety hazard.

Pickets will scatter tacks, roofing nails, childrens' jacks with sharpened points, other sharpened devices to puncture tires at access gates. As this is illegal, they'll use various devices, such as dropping the sharpened devices from holes in their trousers pockets, to hide the act. Observation and Documentation teams must watch for this tactic and document it and the individuals involved.

Strikers also may pretend to be struck and injured by vehicles entering the struck facility or may feign illness at a critical access point.

More violent tactics which can be expected include pickets' palming or concealing in their sleeves flat stones, metal, other sharp objects which they'll then swipe across the vehicle's finish.

If they can't get close to a vehicle, and Observation and Documentation teams seem inattentive or unaware of their act, they may hurl rocks or paint-filled balloons or eggs or similar objects at vehicles or pedestrians. The overt presence of an Observation and Documentation team goes far to discourage this tactic.

The worst violence typical to a strike might occur when strikers attempt to intimidate non-striking employees by forcing them from their cars, overturning cars, breaking car windows. Violent confrontations with police may result in a similar melee.

Violence is far more likely to occur when drinking is a part of picket line activities or when pickets have been drinking before beginning picket line duties. Drink can bolster courage, ease inhibitions, increase belligerence. Observation and Documentation teams must pick up the first signs of drinking on the picket line. It always means trouble.

Observation and Documentation teams also should be alert for any signs of weapons in the hands of strikers: hand guns, shotguns, slingshots, billy clubs or saps, switch-blade knives. Report these instances to police and let them handle it.

Apart from the picket line, violence also is possible at non-striking employees' homes. Paint will be sprayed on houses or pavements, windows broken, gasoline poured on lawns and set afire, vehicles' windows broken, wires cut, gas tanks sabotaged with sand or sugar. The security staff must document these incidents and assist local police in their investigation of them if necessary.

I present the worst side of picket activities. There is a far better side when individuals protest in orderly fashion for rights they believe legitimately theirs. Unfortunately, these better instances are the exception rather than the rule.

If the security staff can maintain a calm, professional attitude at all times; deal with strike leaders and management officials in a firm but courteous and always professional and impartial manner; and always clearly be prepared to document and prosecute any illegal or disorderly acts, chances are that most individuals involved in the argument will behave as they should.

Then the best side of picket line activities will be evident and, when the dispute is resolved, both sides will go back to work with a lot less bitterness in their mouths and hearts.

CHAPTER 19

BOMB THREATS

A prolonged strike, particularly a bitter one, sooner or later will include the threat or actual use of bombs, incendiary devices or similar destructive weapons against the struck company's property or the threat of harm to management figures.

In most cases these threats are only threats and will not be carried out. No threat of this type, however, can be ignored. Each must be assessed on its own merits and in light of what has gone before. If these especially violent tactics have not been used in earlier strikes, they probably will not be used in this one. If they have been used before, using one now will be that much easier, hence more likely.

The central switchboard operator, personnel manning the General Operations Center or the Security Operations Center, department heads or supervisors working during the strike should be oriented on the proper handling of bomb threat calls, threat assessing, emergency procedures to include bomb searches.

Bomb threat checklists, similar in content to the one shown at the end of this chapter, should be available at all times near phones likely to be used for these calls.

If a bomb threat call is received, the person receiving it should take the following actions:

a. Keep talking with the caller. Seem interested, friendly, not biased toward the caller. It may be necessary to pretend that the telephone line is garbled or that the receiver of the call does not understand and must have information repeated—all to keep the caller talking while the listener evaluates the information he is receiving. He must get all the information he can from the caller, particularly: Where is the bomb? What does it look like? What kind of bomb is it (incendiary, explosive, etc.)? When is it set to detonate?

As the call continues, the person receiving it should make notes. It is very important that he recall the exact wording of the caller's basic message because it not only may locate and identify the explosive device for defusing but it also may indicate whether the threat is real or not. For example, if the caller cannot identify the company or the building in which the bomb allegedly has been planted, it probably is not there at all.

b. If possible, and without disturbing the caller, the listener should alert another operator or supervisor to quietly listen to the conversation.

c. Complete the bomb threat checklist immediately after the call and as thoroughly as possible.

d. When the call is completed, the listener should notify his immediate supervisor and all individuals on the emergency notification list (which should be available with the bomb threat checklist). If a listed individual does not immediately respond to the call, he should not wait for that individual but go on notifying others, then return to that individual later.

e. Do not discuss the threatening call with any other individual. Reporters and other outsiders should not be given any information on the bomb threat unless that is done by the company's designated public information official. The term itself should not be used to anyone other than the authorized individuals cited above.

Reporters or other outsiders should not be allowed on the facility during a bomb threat emergency; only local police, bomb disposal specialists, emergency personnel should be admitted.

The Security Director or, in his absence, the senior security staff member on duty in the Security Operations Center, is responsible for the following:

a. Assuring notification of all individuals on the company's official emergency notification list; notifying proper police and other emergency agencies.

b. Directing and supervising a search of the facilities involved.

c. Directing and supervising evacuation of the facility if necessary. The decision to evacuate should be made by the senior company official present, with the advice of the Security Director, not automatically by the Security Director.

d. Directing and supervising reoccupation of the facility after the bomb threat has ended. The basic decision to reoccupy a threatened facility should be made by the senior company official present, on advice of the Security Director.

Following any evacuation of a threatened facility, if the facility is declared safe for reentry during the working shift, the facility should be reoccupied. This discourages future false alarms.

If the alleged detonation time is imminent (few minutes), and the "bomb's" location is given by the caller, the area concerned should be evacuated until a search is completed. If time permits, careful analysis of the credibility of the threat should be done before an evacuation decision is reached. If the facility is evacuated, whether for a real or simulated bomb, the perpetrator has accomplished his basic purpose of disrupting work.

All calls activating bomb threat emergency plans should be as brief as possible to keep lines free and to expedite emergency notification procedures. The line on which the bomb threat was received should be kept free as the individual who made the first call might call again with additional information.

The Director of Security should assure that a log of all communications and other happenings is begun as soon as possible and that the log is maintained throughout the emergency.

Use of two-way radios should be discontinued within the threatened facility until the bomb threat is resolved as it could set off an electrically detonated device.

Depending on the time available and other factors, the initial evacuation decision may have to be made by the senior security supervisor present. As company managers reach the Security Operations Center, however, responsibility for that decision automatically passes to them. The basic rule, however, is that, if in doubt, evacuate.

Employees should take immediate personal affects with them, leaving cabinets and drawers, all doors slightly open to minimize blast effects. If the bomb is located, personnel should not be evacuated through that area (use different exits, different stairwells, etc.). If the facility is multistory, evacuation should be made to at least two (2) floors below the located or suspected bomb location.

Time permitting, one hour as a guide, search of floors cited in the bomb threat would be conducted by teams of employees under the supervision of the security staff. Employees accustomed to working in a particular area should be used, where possible, to search that area as they'd be most likely to notice a suspicious or foreign object (*e.g.*, unexplained length of pipe on the floor of a work area, carton in a rest room, package behind fire extinguishers, etc.). Bomb searchers should listen, divide the area or room into sectors, search one sector at a time, search from the floor up to the ceiling, notify the Security Operations Center as a room is cleared.

Suspicious objects should not be touched by employees. They should summon help from the Security Operations Center which will be in immediate contact with law enforcement agencies or Army demolition teams trained in handling explosive devices. All examination, transport, disposition of possible bombs or incendiary devices must be left to agencies trained in bomb disposal techniques.

The first supervisor on the scene of a detonated device should report it immediately to the Security Operations Center then stand by to direct medical evacuation and damage control measures.

The chances of a struck facility receiving a bomb threat or similar warning are high during a bitter labor dispute. In most cases, they will not materialize into an actual bomb situation. No one, however, can afford to take that chance. The Security Director should have bomb threat emergency plans prepared and rehearsed by appropriate individuals of his and the company's staffs. In a strike situation, supervisors must be briefed on handling bomb threat emergencies. With that preparation, even if the threat is legitimate, the risk of harm to individuals or to the facility is lessened.

BOMB THREAT RESPONSE

Your name: _____ Date: _____

Location: _____

Time call received (AM/PM): _____ Extension: _____

Exact words of caller: _____

_____

_____

Person caller requested: _____

I said: _____

_____

_____

WHERE is it located (record exact words)? _____

_____

WHEN will it explode (record exact words)? _____

_____

WHAT does it look like (record exact words)? _____

_____

WHAT kind of bomb is it (incendiary, explosive) (record exact words)?

_____

WHO is the caller (record exact words)? _____

   Address? _____

   Organization? _____ Phone number? _____

Other statements: _____

_____

Time caller hung up (AM/PM): _____

The caller's:

   Sex: Male _____ Female _____ Age _____

   Voice: Fast _____ Slow _____ Distinct _____ Disguised _____

   Language: English _____ Foreign (identify if possible) _____

         Educated _____ Simple _____ Profanity _____

   Tone: Loud _____ Soft _____ Harsh _____

   Accent: Local _____ Regional (identify) _____

   Manner: Calm _____ Angry _____ Emotional _____ Laughing _____

         Crying _____ Deliberate _____

   I can _____ cannot _____ imitate unusual characteristics of the

caller's voice: _____

The caller's voice was _____ was not _____ familiar to me:

_____

Background noises: _____

_____

_____

   Local call _____ Long distance _____

I notified:

Company: _____ _____

_____

Police: _____ Fire _____

Others: _____

Signed: _____ Date _____ Time _____

CHAPTER 20

SECURITY STRIKE PLAN

No matter how well organized and well drilled a Security Department's or other management staff's operations may be, in a strike situation the staffs operating a struck facility will find themselves playing a whole new ball game.

The facility itself will change in many ways. Not all buildings and areas will be used. Those not used may be shuttered and locked, creating foot and vehicle traffic problems and requiring new procedures for distribution of supplies, raw material, finished goods. Hours of operation, times for shift changes, even procedures for those shift changes (traffic, parking, time clocks, etc.) will change. Handling of waste and salvage material may be considerably altered by the emergency. There may be new and larger storage areas. Shipping and receiving procedures probably will change drastically.

Most important, individuals responsible for key functions at the struck facility will change. Supervisors probably will be asked to perform more than their usual supervisory functions, to handle new and strange areas. They certainly can count on less help from their staffs because those staffs may all be casualties of the labor dispute. If that is so, those supervisors must pitch in and get their own hands dirty, performing menial jobs usually delegated to subordinates. And they may not have worked that way for some time. It will be a new and strange experience to them.

Add to this confusion the uncertainty and anxiety resulting from the strike. Non-striking employees, supervisors, managers will be concerned about possible physical danger to themselves or to their personal property (vehicles while crossing picket lines, their private residences). Although they may want to present a calm and strong image to others, they're going to have personal misgivings. So far as the strikers are concerned, they'll want to carry water on both shoulders. To their bosses, they'll want to seem "good company men and women." That is, loyal to the company in the current dispute. They'll have strong personal ties with certain striking employees, however, and will have to live with those individuals for a long time after the strike ends. They'd rather do nothing that would be remembered as to their personally opposing the strike.

These changes in the physical layout of the struck facility and in its operations, in supervisors' duties and in their emotional involvement with striking employees, are bound to affect supervisors' concentration on keeping the plant operating as peacefully as possible and as efficiently as possible until the strike ends.

For all these reasons and simply to reduce internal confusion as much as possible, a written Security Strike Plan is needed. It will be an annex to the company's General Strike Plan but, because it affects so many facets of company operations, it probably will be the most critical portion of that overall strike management plan.

Prepared under the direction of the Director of Security, the Security Strike Plan should be a comprehensive, concise, workable statement of all the policies the security staff will enforce and the procedures and activities by which they will do it.

Where possible, it should incorporate policies and procedures already in effect. The security staff and other employees already will be familiar with these policies and operations. The least changes to accommodate strike-generated matters, however, the better. And those changes should be spelled-out in detail—not in generalities but in specific detail. The Security Strike Plan should include guidance on present policies and elaboration on those that are changed or added.

The entire plan should be organized and presented in a clear, logical manner affording quick and easy reference. It does little good to have an impressively thick document in fancy cover if the staff can't find a specific item it needs and needs in a hurry. The plan must be logically organized, tabbed, indexed.

Its general wording should be lean. It must be specific enough to provide detailed guidance (rather than a general statement of policy which leaves implementation almost entirely to the imagination, discretion or whim of the individual responsible for carrying it out) so that the entire operation is coordinated, yet not be cumbersome. The sinews of intent must not be lost in the flesh of ten pounds of ornate composition. Keep it short, simple, to the point.

The Security Strike Plan might include the following items:

a. Company's Strike Mission, *e.g.,* to continue operations at some specified level while attempting to end the work stoppage as soon as possible.

 b. Company Emergency Staff's Mission & Organization.

  (1) Mission.

  (2) Location of various staff members.

  (3) Duties and responsibilities of individuals.

  (4) Chain-of-command.

 c. Strike Mission & Organization of Security Staff.

  (1) Mission.

   (a) Preserve Order.

   (b) Protect personnel and property from harm.

   (c) Assist continuation of operations and provide secure working environment at all company locations.

   (d) Cooperate with local authorities.

   (e) Conduct investigations to determine causes of incidents, individuals responsible, provide documentation for legal purposes.

   (f) Provide observation and documentation concerning disorder and illegal acts for legal purposes.

  (2) Assignment of Security Personnel.

   (a) Proprietary Security Officers.

   (b) Contract Security Officers.

   (c) Investigators.

   (d) Observation & Documentation Teams.

   (e) Security Operations Center; Security Control Center.

   (f) Consultants.

 d. Principles for Guidance of Supervisors.

  (1) Use of proprietary/contract Security Officer mix.

  (2) Dealing with striking and non-striking employees during work stoppage.

  (3) Legal principles.

  (4) Picket line operations.

  (5) Observation and documentation.

  (6) Dealing with local police and other agencies.

  (7) Dealing with public media, local community.

 e. Continuation of existing Standing Operating Procedures.

 f. Changes to existing Standing Operating Procedures.

 g. New Standing Operating Procedures.

 h. Guard Operations.

  (1) Staff assignments (supervisors, duties, teams, etc.).

(2) Shift assignments; post assignments.

(3) Patrol Rounds (specific routes, General/Special Orders).

    (a) Foot.

    (b) Vehicle.

    (c) Fixed Posts.

    (d) Detex Clocks.

(4) Logistics support.

(5) Reports.

  i. Security Control Center.

(1) Mission.

(2) Staffing.

(3) Location.

(4) Logistics support.

(5) Reports; coordination with other operations centers.

  j. Security Operations Center.

(1) Mission.

(2) Staffing.

(3) Location.

(4) Logistics support.

(5) Reports; coordination with other operations centers.

  k. Closed Circuit Television Coverage.

(1) Cameras.

    (a) Locations.

    (b) Assigned coverage.

(2) Monitoring.

    (a) Assignments of monitors.

    (b) Monitoring procedures.

    (c) Response procedures.

(3) Maintenance.

    (a) Scheduled maintenance; emergency repairs.

    (b) Scheduled testing procedures.

(4) Reports.

  l. Alarm Coverage.

    (a) Locations; types.

    (b) Monitoring procedures.

    (c) Maintenance; emergency repairs; scheduled testing procedures.

    (d) Reports.

  m. Observation and Documentation Teams.

(1) Mission.
(2) Legal principles.
    (a) Contact with employees, local police.
    (b) Legal and illegal strike activities.
    (c) Elements of proof.
(3) Assignments (individuals to teams, teams to posts).
(4) Equipment (cite by team, use, accountability).
(5) Logistics support.
(6) Reports.
n. Communications.
    (1) Telephone numbers.
        (a) Emergency Operations Centers.
        (b) Chain-of-Command.
        (c) Emergency Staff Departments.
        (d) Police.
        (e) Fire.
        (f) Medical.
        (g) Bomb.
        (h) Vendors and other support units.
        (i) Contract agencies.
    (2) Beeper numbers for key individuals, as cited above.
    (3) Radio nets (Operations Centers, guards, Observation and Documentation teams, local police, etc.).
o. Government Security Requirements (if applicable).
p. Access Controls.
    (1) Emergency identification card system.
    (2) Gate assignments (vehicle, pedestrian, contractor, etc.).
    (3) Pedestrian and vehicle security check points and procedures.
    (4) Visitor controls.
    (5) Handling trespassers.
    (6) Restricted areas.
    (7) Traffic and parking patterns.
q. Emergency Procedures.
    (1) Fire.
    (2) Bomb.
    (3) Natural Disaster, etc.
r. Logistics.
    (1) Personnel support (dining, sleeping, bathing, medical, recreation facilities, uniforms, laundry, public phones, etc.).

(2) Special equipment (issuance, accountability, maintenance).

(3) Maintenance (scheduled and emergency).

(4) Fuel.

(5) Vehicle control.

s. Overlays, maps, photomaps, plans, routes, etc., giving visual representation of facility(s) and of specific procedures to be in effect during strike emergency.

For maximum usefulness, the plan has to be rather widely disseminated. For example, copies, or extracts of pertinent portions of the Security Strike Plan, probably should be given to the following individuals:

a. Senior company officials on premises during strike.

b. Labor Relations or Industrial Relations Director.

c. Company's legal representative.

d. Supervisor of General Operations Center.

e. Supervisor of Security Control Center.

f. Supervisor of Security Operations Center.

g. Shipping and Receiving supervisor (extracts).

h. Transportation supervisor (extracts).

i. Senior police commander.

j. Senior member of any government regulatory agencies involved in work dispute.

Much of the contents of the Security Strike Plan may become known to the strikers or to other individuals having no real need to know those details. The Security Director should make every effort to lessen this risk, but it will remain. Some slippage will occur. With this necessarily wide distribution, it will be difficult to keep details of the plan from someone who really wants to know. It does no real harm, however, for striking employees to know that the security force is well-organized, alert, prepared, assigned an aggressive policy of preventing or containing violence, damage or other illegal acts; identifying perpetrators; assisting the company in its stated policy of prosecuting law breakers.

Certain sensitive matters, however, such as confidential telephone numbers or radio codes, alert notification procedures, should be limited to those who really have need for them. No one—not the chief executive of the company nor any other executive—really has need for that type information unless he actually plans to be involved in its operations. For example, if the number of the outside line to the Security Operations Center is widely distributed and falls into the wrong hands, that line could be monitored for sensitive information or, in some instances, denied use by someone's calling it from another phone then not replacing the calling telephone on its cradle after the Security Operations Center phone is replaced on its cradle.

The plan must be current. Dusting off a plan prepared several years before and which now contains erroneous information about the facility or about the organization or operations of the security staff can only cause confusion, dismay, lack of confidence. If it is not current, make it current before issuing it to individuals who will be responsible for carrying out its directives.

As the tactical situation changes (weather, company plans, picket tactics, etc.), it may be necessary to change part of the Security Strike Plan to keep it current. Those changes should be put in writing and issued to each holder of the original plan. That must be done concurrently with execution of any changes or as promptly as absolutely possible afterward.

In pre-strike planning all contingencies cannot be foreseen, nor can they be provided for. To do so would make an impossibly cumbersome document anyway. The more a basic plan can be in being before the strike, however, the fewer improvisations will be necessary after it begins. This goes a long way toward lessening the chance of mistakes, unwanted confrontations. Certainly it goes a long way toward helping the Security Director meet his responsibilities in a strike situation.

CHAPTER 21

WILDCAT STRIKES

This text primarily focuses on economic strikes, legal strikes by employees to gain particular job benefits and which are begun with the required warning notices in a legal manner. Economic strikes usually are not begun overnight. The striking union requires time to prepare them. The Security Director usually will have some warning that there is real danger of an economic strike, hence some time to prepare his defenses against its effects.

Sometimes, however, that is not the case. He is not that fortunate. Some strikes occur with little or no warning. Typical would be the wildcat strike. A wildcat strike is a strike which normally does not have the approval of the union, which may be in violation of a no-strike contract provision, which almost certainly will violate federal or state laws in not providing the time warnings required. As such, unless they are to protest a valid management's unfair labor practice, they are illegal.

Because there is little warning before a "wildcat," "quickie," "illegal," or "outlaw" strike, the Security Director should always have a good idea of his company's overall strike management policies. Armed with this, and if he has carefully trained his security staff and developed standing operating procedures for strike security, he may be hard pressed but is going to come through the strike emergency all right. That means his company will come through it with minimum disruption, minimum violence, minimum bad feelings regardless of how the dispute is resolved.

Whether his pre-strike planning is complete or not, if a strike occurs, the Security Director has three major objectives:

a. Prevent or minimize violence or other illegal acts which disrupt company operations and harm personnel or property.

b. Observe, recognize, document significant happenings.

c. Identify strike leaders and individuals involved in illegal strike activities.

If a wildcat strike occurs, management should attempt to keep its supervisors as calm and as busy as possible. They should not abandon the work site to the strikers but, insofar as they can, should attempt to continue their daily operations while making it possible for employees to return to work if they wish to. If supervisors abandon the scene, workers who wish to work won't be able to do so. Usually the wildcat strike will involve only a small part of the work force. With skill it can be contained to that limited group. Other workers may continue with minimal interruption from the striking group. Another reason for supervisors' not abandoning work areas caught in a wildcat strike is that, if they do abandon them, management will not be in position to know what is happening at the strike scene. Finally, supervisors must never voluntarily give up their authority on the job.

Supervisors should not attempt to negotiate or discuss the issues involved in a wildcat strike—leave that to designated company negotiators trained in that task. The same applies to the security staff, only more so. Security personnel must maintain a neutral, professional, peacekeeping role and leave the arguing to others.

The security staff should adjust their resources and procedures to insure solid security coverage of the departments or areas affected by the strike. This may mean immediate organization and assignment of Observation and Documentation teams to observe, document, report all significant happenings.

Wildcat strikes often result in disciplinary action against strike leaders or participants in illegal work stoppages. Management must prove its case, however, and that is where the work of the Observation and Documentation team is so important. Team leaders must recognize illegal acts and be prompt to document them by video tape, still photos, audio tape, interview of witnesses, their own written reports.

The security staff must recognize and identify leaders of the illegal strike activity. They should watch for such things as an individual's waving or calling others off the job; shutting down or damaging equipment; being the first to stop work; directing other striking employees to establish picket lines; demonstrating against supervisors; confronting or threatening supervisors.

In observing and reporting these activities and individuals involved in them, the security teams should work in pairs if possible; should make detailed notes during or immediately after observing the incident; should record all the facts, paying particular attention to the exact location and time of significant events. They must be careful to delineate between personally observed or heard facts and hearsay reports. If their reports include personal opinions, they should be labeled as such.

Security staffs should recognize and identify members of the facility's recognized union and document their activities during the illegal strike. These union members' involvement or lack of involvement in the work stoppage, and their attitudes toward it, may accurately reflect their local's attitude toward it. This would be helpful in planning strike management strategy and in supporting a request for injunctive relief.

Although a strike is called with little or no warning and perhaps without the knowledge of the union itself, it still may be a legal strike, hence legally protected and not subject to court-ordered relief. An example might be an impromptu work stoppage over a serious safety problem. Whether the stoppage is legal is not the primary concern of the Security Director. His job, whatever the cause of the stoppage, is to restore order and to document any illegal acts performed during the strike.

The rights of an employer to discipline employees involved in a wildcat strike depend upon the legality of the strike itself. When it occurs under a collective bargaining agreement which prohibits strikes (and if the strike is not over an unfair labor practice by management), the company's right to fire striking employees generally is recognized by arbitrators and courts. Usually, however, the employer must establish clear proof of individuals' participation in illegal acts. Often that is not easy to do. That is why the role of the security staff is so important. They'll have to establish that proof.

During a wildcat strike, there probably will not be time or need to establish a completely operational General Operations Center. Perhaps not even a Security Operations Center. It also may be that the Security Director will be assigned responsibility for all aspects, other than negotiations, of controlling the limited work stoppage. If the strike continues for several days and more company functions become affected by it, however, both operations centers may be activated. The Security Director must look toward this possibility and plan to meld his security

operations into the company's overall strike management plan, relin-
quishing his own overall authority and focusing upon strike security
portions of that overall plan.

Regardless of the duration of the strike, its intensity, its breadth, its
nature, the more the Security Director has used "quiet times" to prepare
himself and his staff to handle strike emergencies, the better they'll be
able to cope with one in whatever form it may take.

CHAPTER 22

POST-STRIKE OPERATIONS

Historically, most strikes are settled when real changes in position and attitude occur—changes brought about by economic pressure on both sides and by individual employees' genuine wishes to return to work rather than by the persuasion and good will of either management or labor. If such persuasion and good will had been possible in the first place, the strike probably would not have occurred at all. Compromise of strike issues ordinarily comes from internal pressure on both management and union leaders rather than by the persuasive skills of negotiators for either side. That fact of life leaves room for bitterness among participants.

However the dispute is resolved, hopefully during the strike the Security Director has been able to keep both sides from turning to violence or has prevented acts which might have harmed individuals or company or non-striking employees' property. Once done, those acts can't be undone. Recollection of them delays the reconciliation process.

The relationship between the company and its union, between negotiators for both sides in the dispute, between employees caught on one side or the other, will be as sensitive immediately after the strike as it was during it. The signing of a negotiated settlement won't immediately soothe bad feelings begun or exacerbated during the strike. Antagonisms always present during a dispute may have been further aggravated by picket line incidents or other confrontations or by management's disciplining individuals for acts committed during the strike. That antagonism won't be quickly forgotten.

When the strike ends, however, it's time for the reconciliation process to do its work. The security staff can play a key role in it. The individual Security Officer at the facility's main gate the morning after the strike ends will be the first company representative returning workers will encounter. It is very important that that individual behave in a highly professional manner, maintaining a calm, friendly but reserved demeanor and doing nothing that would further irritate an already tense situation.

191

As for management, its best approach in a post-strike situation is to resume operations as fully, as effectively, as quickly as possible. The busier individuals are the quicker everyone will see a return to normalcy. And they'll have less chance to dwell on real or imagined antagonisms fostered by the strike.

Managers, particularly lower level supervisors, must insist that terms of the settlement be scrupulously followed by both sides. The security staff must be alerted to any specific facets of that settlement which they would be expected to monitor, as in revised safety procedures or changes to company rules. Deviations from strike settlement agreements must be immediately addressed before the situation worsens.

Another immediate post-strike responsibility for the Security Director is assuring proper closing of the operations centers in an efficient and effective manner. Any remaining reports must be prepared for analysis and for historical and legal purposes. Sensitive documents, photographs, other supporting material should be screened and marked for destruction or secured storage. Certain strike reports (identification and activities of strike leaders, union strike tactics, community involvement, police reports, intelligence reports and sources, similar information) are sensitive and must be handled that way. If they no longer have value, they should be destroyed. If they still have value, they should be stored in a safe and secure place.

. The Security Director also must insure that all equipment and supplies used by his department during the strike are properly accounted for, given necessary maintenance, and either properly stored or, if borrowed or leased, returned to their proper owners. Much of the equipment will be of a highly technical nature, usually involving considerable expense. Supplies of film, video tape, audio cassettes, batteries are expensive. During a strike, costs may be forgotten or temporarily overlooked. With the strike ended, however, it's time to come back to real life. Every dollar counts. All equipment and supplies must be accounted for. Maintenance neglected during the press of other matters must be completed before equipment is returned to storage. Damaged items must be repaired or replaced so that the department will be ready if another emergency occurs. Sooner or later, it probably will.

When the immediate tasks of phasing down emergency operations and properly accounting for equipment and supplies are completed, the Security Director and his staff should reexamine the entire strike experience and their individual roles in it. This should be done as soon as possible. Memories fade. Lessons learned during the strike must not be forgotten. More important, if there is another strike, mistakes must not be repeated. Good managers profit by every experience.

There are many lessons to be learned from any strike. The Security Director must determine whether his Security Strike Plan worked as it should have worked. Were mistakes made? What were they? How might it have been done better? Was manpower adequate for the job at hand? Was it properly used? Did notification procedures work satisfactorily? Did the security staff respond properly to new or unexpected situations? How could those situations have been handled better? Was observation and documentation adequate for legal purposes? Should more Observation and Documentation teams have been created? Were they adequately trained? Did equipment work satisfactorily? If not, what equipment was lacking or what should be repaired or replaced? How well did the security staff, particularly its members working in the Security Operations Center, coordinate their activities with other management functions? Which individuals performed well? Which did not? How might that be improved? How effective was police support? How might it be improved? How might the Security Director address each of these questions to improve his department's performance?

Before answering these questions and before preparing a formal, after-action report for his department, he should sit in an informal, open, relaxed session with key members of the security staff. During this session he must encourage individuals to take part in a free discussion of what went well, what did not go well, and why the difference. Just as important as gleaning their thoughts on the overall operation is his encouraging each one to feel that his own contributions to protecting the company have been noted and appreciated.

These discussions and his own thoughtful, professional overall appraisal of his department's performance should result in improvement to the Security Director's Security Strike Plan and probably will contribute much to the company's overall strike management strategy should both be needed again. Unless they do, a large part of his department's experience during the emergency may be wasted. The same mistakes probably will occur again in any future strike.

Incorporating lessons learned from the strike experience in an improved Security Strike Plan won't prevent another strike. Nor will it cause one. If one does occur, however, the Security Director will be better able to cope with it. And so will his company.

CHAPTER 23

SUMMARY: ANATOMY OF A STRIKE

In the following account, names of locales, companies, unions, individuals, certain dates have been changed. Incidents relating to the strike, however, are true. It is an accurate rendering of a strike which actually occurred several years ago.

Bridgeville is a pleasant town bordering a large urban area in New York State. Its population is 17,000, of widely mixed racial and economic backgrounds. Law enforcement problems are typical to an urban area but normally are not considered severe. Bridgeville has good school and library systems, fifteen churches, a broad mix of industry and business, some of which spilled over from the neighboring city.

The largest industry in Bridgeville is Empire Pharmaceuticals whose 500 fenced acres include the company headquarters, research facility, manufacturing plant. Empire Pharmaceuticals manufactures pharmaceuticals, biologicals and antibiotics. It employs about 4300 people.

In 1979 Local 902 of the International Chemical Workers Union represented Empire's production and maintenance employees—about 1800 workers, 800 of whom were members of the union. The company had no strikes between 1952–1962. In 1962 there was an illegal strike which lasted five days and ended without the company's being charged with any grievance or unfair labor practice. Union and company then kept the peace for fifteen years until a 1977 strike which lasted 103 days. The subsequent peace lasted only until September, 1979 when a five months' strike began.

The 1977 and 1979 strikes resulted from the union's demands for a Union shop, company-wide bargaining on pensions and insurance, absolute seniority on all job movements, cost-of-living clauses to all union contracts. Both strikes were very bitter. In less than two years (1977–1979) Empire employees were on strike for over eight months. They did not

194

win their objectives and their losses in wages during the strikes probably never will be made up. We focus on the September, 1979 strike.

In the spring of 1979, Empire's management concluded that a strike at the contract expiration date (1 September) was likely and that it would be a long and bitter one. There were many indications.

After the 1977 strike, some union members, especially the militant ones, continued to show hostility toward the company and toward fellow employees who had returned to work during the strike. This agitation fostered a high level of tension in the plant. This was frequently reported during 1977–1979 by first-line supervisors and by the security staff. The slogan "Hit the Line in '79," popular during the earlier strike, was revived and appeared, along with "Sock-it-to-em" stickers, in many places throughout the plant and on highway signs outside the company entrances. The "Sock-it-to-em" phrase also appeared in union publications.

The November 13, 1978 edition of the Bridgeville Times-Leader featured an article entitled "Outward Calm at Empire Hides Union Bitterness." In the article, Harry Costin, President of Local 902, ICWU, reportedly stated, "Things will be different next time. We were gentlemen and ladies on the picket line last year, but if we have to strike again you can count on much more militancy." This view was expressed again in a June 21, 1979 article, "If there is to be a strike this year, that will be up to the company. If there is one, we serve notice to one and all that it will *not* be conducted as it was in '77. This time it's not going to be easy to cross the picket line."

Tension among employees also was heightened by competition among several unions to recruit Empire employees. In November 1978 the International Brotherhood of Teamsters handed out organizing pamphlets and signature cards at the plant's main gate. This was followed by an equally aggressive membership drive by the United Mine Workers of America, District 45, which handbilled plant entrances on seven separate occasions during the spring of 1979. During this entire period the Independent Industrial Union, a locally formed group of dissident employees, also campaigned within the plant. Local 902, ICWU, counterattacked its rival unions with its own campaign, more strident and promising to do whatever was necessary at expiration of the current contract (September 1, 1979) to win huge gains for its members. The one-upmanship had to mean trouble at the bargaining table and beyond.

Supervisors and members of the security staff frequently reported overhearing workers' comments that the union would strike if it felt it could not win its goals at the bargaining table. Discrete inquiries also revealed feelers by Local 902, ICWU, to its national headquarters and among other Bridgeville area unions for their support should a strike vote be taken.

Union positions at contract negotiations became firmer, more strident. All the while union shop stewarts throughout the Empire plant handed management a rash of petty, sometimes flippant grievances. Certain shop stewarts, it seemed, were agitating for the sake of agitating.

The company began its own preparations. Stocks were inventoried, stockpiling begun to provide for six months' use. Equipment and building maintenance was expedited. Managers began to review their portions of the company's overall strike management plan and to consider individuals to fill critical roles if a strike began.

Empire's Security Director was handed a full plate of responsibility in strike planning. He was charged with coordinating the entire staff's revision of the overall plan, in addition to updating and improving his own Security Annex to that plan. He was to insure readiness of the security staff to handle strike emergencies; to review emergency plans; to secure necessary additional security equipment; to work with Empire's legal counsel and his own staff to assure gathering of evidence concerning property damage or harm or threats of harm to individuals during the labor confrontation. He also would be the company's primary liaison with all law enforcement agencies and with the Department of Defense (Empire held several defense contracts). He would be responsible for setting up a General Operations Center as well as his own Security Operations Center.

As the strike deadline neared, the company decided it would attempt to operate as normally as possible during any strike. Management realized this stand could cause mass picketing, increase the chance of violence and harassment, and poison the bargaining atmosphere (hence prolong the strike). It also could mean prolonged bitterness after the strike ended. Still, with more than 1,000 non-union office employees, a like number of supervisory and professional people, and the likelihood that at least some non-bargaining unit employees would cross picket lines to return to work, they'd be able to operate the plant. And Empire's continuing to operate despite the union's best effort would have tremendous psychological impact upon the strikers.

In hopes it might shorten the strike, the company decided to discontinue all strikers' insurance plans during a strike. It realized, however, that this would have limited effect in light of the militant attitude evident in the union and the fact that in New York State strikers could draw unemployment compensation after seven weeks' without work, for whatever reason. No one doubted that the strike probably would be a long and bitter one.

Empire planned back-up transportation for working employees by the rail line normally used to supply the plant and by helicopter flights from the local airport. Resupply and shipment of finished goods primarily would be by railroad with limited use of interstate trucking transshipped into and from the plant by local carriers from the nearby city.

Three gates would be used, the others securely padlocked and patrolled. The large main gate, equipped for vehicle and pedestrian entrance/exit, would be the primary gate during strike operations. A smaller vehicular gate at the far end of the facility would be designated for contractor use only. The railroad gate would be a third entrance/exit. Because of its criticality in shipping/receiving operations and possible use to transport workers into the plant, the railroad gate demanded extra security coverage.

The Security Director coordinated requirements with the firm's legal counsel, then planned six, two-man teams of observers and recorders/photographers to cover plant entrances. One would be stationed at a long central observation point on the roof of the main production building. Other teams, stationed in two-way radio equipped Blazers, would be stationed at each of the three gates. The Blazers afforded cover for team members and provided for quick redeployment.

The Security Director also arranged for a private security firm to provide two more observer/photographer/investigative teams to operate outside Empire's perimeter. All teams would be briefed by the company's legal counsel and directed from the Security Operations Center.

During August the Security Director met with local, county and state police as well as with DOD representatives. All pledged support to maintain the peace.

Two groups of reliable, mature, long-time Empire employees agreed to act as picket line testers.

Additional security equipment included extra movie and television cameras with telephoto lens, high-powered binoculars, a night-sighting device, five two-way radios, a CB radio for the Security Operations Center, extra floodlights (provided by the Bridgeville Power Company) at the main entrance. Later, these extra floodlights proved to be critically important for proper observation and identification and were replaced by additional permanent lighting.

A tow truck was rented and brought into the plant and one company truck was equipped with towing devices to remove any equipment stalled at gates. Electromagnets were installed on a Security Department scooter for use in sweeping metal from entrance roadways. Later, this proved to be ineffective and handsweeping was necessary.

Four portable generators with high-intensity floodlights were leased to provide emergency floodlighting. Two large privet hedges at the main entrance were trimmed to allow an unrestricted view of picketing at that critical gate at all times. Perimeter fences were repaired. A gap, long used as an "unofficial" gate by workers, was sealed and marked with "No Trespassing" signs.

At 11 p.m., August 29, 1979, one hour before the strike deadline, the company's Security Strike Plan was put in full effect. All security staff members, not then on duty, were notified to come into the plant and to plan to remain there for the duration of the strike. They'd work twelve-hour shifts, sixteen men each. All guard emergency posts were manned. Personal vehicles of employees scheduled to remain in the plant over the Labor Day weekend if a strike occurred were brought within the fenced area to a well-lit, secure parking area. Clear zones along the entire facility perimeter were established and maintained during the strike.

Intelligence reports indicated that the union would place a picket line at the main gate soon after midnight, with picketing at all three entrances the following morning and mass picketing on Tuesday following the holiday weekend.

At approximately 11:45 p.m., individuals began to collect in front of the Empire Diner across from the main entrance. The group swelled. At 12:05 a.m. a Ford station wagon, bearing Local 902 officials and equipped with a loudspeaker, appeared on Main Street. It traveled up and down the length of Empire Pharmaceuticals broadcasting that Local 902, ICWU, was on strike and directing the group in front of the diner to form a picket line. About sixty individuals immediately crossed the street and began to block the main entrance. The station wagon then entered the plant and circled the North parking lot and the night production area. The strike again was announced and all union members were directed to leave the plant. Many employees immediately left adjacent buildings for vehicles or the pedestrian gate. They'd been ready and waiting.

About ten minutes later, pickets attempted to block the first car attempting to enter the facility. A dozen pickets immediately began assaulting a lone Bridgeville police officer who was attempting to help the driver. Three other Bridgeville policemen, who then moved to help him, also were assaulted by masses of pickets. The police officers were knocked or pushed to the ground and swarmed over in such numbers that observers within the plant could not see the police officers on the street.

The Security Operations Center immediately notified the Bridgeville Police Department. Within moments a small detachment of police reinforcements arrived. The general riot, however, was not checked until another detachment of police reinforcements, some local and some state police in full riot gear, arrived some twenty minutes later.

Police arrested ten strikers, among them Joseph De Carlo, the ICWU International representative and chief strike negotiator, seven Empire employees who were in the massed picket line, and two local youths, not related to the plant staff but who'd been loitering near the Bridgeville Diner and joined the melee after it began. Police emergency riot calls had sounded at all police departments in the county and by 1 a.m. almost every county law enforcement agency was represented at the strike scene.

During the riot, scuffling pickets seized weapons, night sticks, caps, badges, radios from police officers. Several police cars were damaged. Four police officers, as well as a number of strikers, required first aid treatment.

During and after the riot, the police were subjected to such verbal abuse as "kill the cops," "kill the scabs," "police brutality." Other vicious name calling and profanity were common.

By 1:30 a.m. the riot was under control. Although the picket line remained noisy, picketing became peaceful except for several flare-ups when additional cars tried to cross the picket line. These were badly scratched by rock and metal bearing strikers, rocked and pounded. Drivers were threatened but, assisted by police, made their way across the picket line. From that time on ten or more policemen were available at the main gate whenever pickets also were there in force.

The main gate picket line, at the height of the riot, exceeded 150 persons. Another crowd, about the same size, apparently not Empire employees but interested local young people and neighborhood residents, watched from across the street. They shouted encouragement to the strikers, obscenties at police. A few joined the melee. Most, however, found it safer to stay on the sidelines.

Several hours later, police strength remained more than fifty officers, while the picket line shrank to less than a dozen people. Picketers seemed discouraged by the prompt and forceful action of the police officers to early picket aggressiveness. Many already expressed disappointment and dissatisfaction with their union leadership. As a number of strike leaders had been arrested, the pickets' reorganization following the riot, and further development of mass picketing was slow, hesitant.

During the remainder of the Labor Day weekend, picket activities at the three gates remained low. Pickets, however, were present in force at all three gates. Other pickets appeared on the Elm Street railroad overpass some fifty yards below the plant.

Based on the early strike violence and on intelligence reports indicating that there would be mass picketing and more violence on Tuesday, the Security Director used the remainder of the weekend to continue his department's preparations.

He met with the Bridgeville Chief of Police, with the Summit County Sheriff, the Commander of the local NY State Police detachment, the FBI Resident Agent and with the field representative of the Defense Supply Agency, DOD. It was unlikely that all these agencies would be involved in strike management activities, but his actions established his department's credibility in seeking to maintain order during the dispute.

Empire's legal representative formally notified the Governor's Office in Albany of the potentially explosive situation at the plant and the Governor then wired Harry Costin, head of Local 902, ICWU, of his personal interest in maintaining order at the facility and enjoining the union leadership to control workers' picket line violence.

The Security Director arranged for four outside professional photographers to be available at 6 a.m. Tuesday. One would provide helicopter-based photo coverage of expected picket line violence. Three additional Observation and Documentation teams were drafted from available company supervisory personnel and supervisors with some knowledge of photography. They might not be needed, but they'd be available.

Emergency messages to all personnel expected to report for work the following Tuesday morning were passed over a supervisor-centered emergency telephone net. The messages updated employees on the strike situation and summarized their earlier briefing on proper conduct while crossing picket lines.

Motion picture film of the riot was helicoptered from the plant for pre-arranged processing. Still photos would be developed at the plant's photo lab. Over the weekend, pickets attempted to stop this helicopter service by burning tar-filled barrels just beyond the plant's perimeter near the helicopter landing area. On one occasion, a photo courier leaving the airport was followed by identified union members. Local police, however, quickly intervened to stop both practices.

On advice of legal counsel, Security Officers would apprehend and detain trespassers but were instructed *not* to talk with them. Local police would make appropriate arrests. Unless the Security Officer saw a clear danger from the trespasser, searching would be left to the police. The Bridgeville Chief of Police requested and received assurance that Empire would file complaints against trespassers. As the strike progressed a number of striking employees would trespass company property. In all but one instance it was to return or pick up personal belongings from company lockers. Individuals apprehended in these cases were cited for misdemeanors. In one instance, an individual was apprehended attempting to damage oil tank drains and subsequently faced criminal charges.

Because of the potential for violence by strikers and the company's aggressive countermeasures, Bridgeville police foresaw more violence after the holiday. They established an emergency communications center in a trailer a block from the plant's main entrance. By Tuesday the union had set up its own trailer headquarters behind the Empire Diner's lot. During the initial weeks of the strike the police emergency center was avoided by union leaders. Later, when tempers cooled somewhat, it served as "neutral ground" for meetings to discuss on-the-spot problems between management and strikers.

Over the weekend, only a handfull of pickets remained at the main gate. Because of this and the continuing presence of a number of police units, Empire employees were permitted to leave the plant with instructions to report early for their Tuesday shifts.

Intelligence reports also indicated that union members were surprised and dismayed at the toughness of local police in their initial confrontation. The arrest and detention of strike leaders over the long weekend pending hearings left picketers disorganized and confused. Many pickets openly expressed disgust with their leadership.

Known militants among the pickets, however, taunted Security Officers with reports of an expected Tuesday motorcade of fifty cars with Teamster reinforcements to permanently block the main entrance. The same sources, watching the plant's maintenance staff sweep the entrance clear of roofing nails, threatened to use "other ways" to puncture vehicle tires. There also was talk of the pickets' banging on sides and roofs of vehicles and possibly turning over or burning a car to attract media attention. None of these threats materialized.

Union leadership protested to news media about the wooden barricades police had established to control traffic at the two vehicle entrances. There also was much talk of "police brutality" at the earlier confrontation, "brutality" the union hoped to see repeated before a TV audience the following day.

Tuesday, however, proved to be surprisingly quiet. The large number of police on hand discouraged violence. Although nearly 400 pickets attempted to block the main entrance, anticipated Teamsters' reinforcements never materialized and a large police contingent discouraged other than vocal harassment. Perhaps most important, a steady drizzle developed early and continued throughout the day. That rain increased the following day and continued, off and on, for the next several days. Soggy strikers lost interest in the plant area.

The International Union's legal staff devoted the week following Labor Day to petitioning the State Supreme Court to limit police action at the plant. When this was rejected, they turned to the Federal Court in the Western District of New York. A week and a half later Judge Thomas Frankel rejected their appeal with a scathing indictment of the violence which already had taken place at Empire Pharmaceuticals and which Empire had fully documented for Judge Frankel's viewing.

Negotiations among the police chief, the town attorney, union and management attorneys resulted in a "gentlemen's agreement" compromise whereby four pickets would be allowed to picket in the area between the police barricades so long as cars were allowed to enter and leave the plant without interference. This "agreement" was not put in writing and the morning it was to have been effected Local 902's president, Harry Costin, rejected it out of hand. The resistance was largely vocal, however, and following the first day's riot at the main gate picketing was for the most part peaceful. Eventually the police replaced their wooden barricades with yellow rubber cones and yellow lanes painted on the roadway. Throughout the strike the union would muster as much strength as possible at the plant's main gate, always insisting on its right to stop all cars from entering or leaving but not pushing that "right" in confrontation with local police on duty.

On Thursday, the 4th, five pickets, two of whom lay down across the main line of the Erie-Lackawana Railroad south of the plant, stopped the train scheduled for the first rail entry into the struck facility. No arrests were made. The train turned back. The following day, when pickets again blocked the track, railroad police requested they move aside. When they did not, local police arrested several pickets. The others moved from the track and the train entered the Empire yard without further trouble. During the early morning hours several days later, unidentified individuals attempted to dynamite a large section of the contested track. The explosive failed to detonate and was discovered by railroad police preparing for a train run that morning. Local FBI agents investigated the incident but no arrests were made. From that point, however, although there were repeated incidents of rocks or other missiles thrown at passing trains from the Elm Street overpass or from massed pickets near the railhead, all scheduled trains entered and left the facility without any real problem.

Payday normally would have come on the Friday following Labor Day. This time it did not. This further sapped the strikers' morale. The union attempted to pay strike benefits but overall funding made it a token gesture. Among striking workers there were increasing signs of discontent with their union leadership. Estimates of picket strength dwindled as the strike wore on. Not more than 120 hardcore pickets were counted on most occasions with perhaps as many as 200 when the weather was pleasant. Fortunately for management, the weather remained very unpleasant for the critical first several weeks of the strike. In spite of the grumbling within their ranks, however, union leaders maintained a tough stance at the bargaining table and picketing continued at all entrances.

Although the presence of police and Empire's documentation teams discouraged physical confrontations at plant entrances, some form of violence marked most of the strike. More than 200 such incidents were reported to the Security Department during the five months' confrontation. These ranged from a telephone bomb threat to an employee's home on the afternoon before the strike began to several alleged or documented sabotage attempts on company property.

More than 400 reports cited damage to cars of employees crossing picket lines, including long scratches on car finishes probably made with can openers. Rocks and glass constantly littered entrance roadways. Most troublesome during the strike were nails or twisted staples thrown on entranceways to destroy vehicles' tires. There were numerous reports of rocks, eggs, urine-filled balloons thrown from pickets' ranks at workers crossing picket lines. One employee suffered severe facial cuts from a rock thrown at her as she entered the main gate. The plant received nine telephone bomb threats. None proved to be true although one appeared legitimate enough to cause temporary closing and evacuation of a large portion of the struck facility.

Employees reported vehicle tires slashed at their homes, spray painting of their homes, gasoline-burned crosses on their lawns. One supervisor's family vehicle was set afire in his driveway. Police were limited in their ability to protect all employees but random patrols at threatened homes discouraged repeat visits.

All reports of violence or other illegal activities were entered in the Security Department's logs, reported to local law enforcement agencies, and, where appropriate, investigated by Empire's security staff. All documentation was coordinated with Empire's legal staff for use in injunctive proceedings or other legal actions.

As the initial, most violent, phase of the strike waned, the security staff settled into performing routine procedures and handling new situations as they developed, cooperating with operating units in the plant to support production, coordinating with local police and state agencies to show strength and vigilance at likely confrontation points.

After several weeks picket lines at plant entrances settled into a pattern of eighteen to twenty pickets at the main entrance, four or five at the railhead and contractor gates. Picket strength usually increased somewhat during shift changes to harass employees entering or leaving the plant. During the nights picket strength dropped to five or six at the main gate, two or three at other entrances. On extremely cold or snowing days the number of pickets at each gate dropped to one or two, sometimes none. After the first days of aggressive confrontation, vehicle and pedestrian entrances were never completely blocked nor were there delays sufficient to warrant attempting to block the picketing altogether.

During the second week, after several striking employees were found inside the plant, emergency ID cards were issued to employees working in the plant and similar emergency vehicle passes were issued to employees of the key emergency group. These emergency identification systems worked well during the remainder of the strike.

The biggest problem from the standpoint of harassment by pickets and the prevention of injury and property damage to employees was that of nails and bent staples and sharpened jacks, strewn on entrance roadways. This nail problem continued on almost a daily basis throughout the strike and largely remained unsolvable. Observers, even those with high-powered binoculars, could not identify individuals dropping the obstacles. Even police officers near the picket lines could not spot individual pickets dropping the sharp objects on the road. Nevertheless they were there and roadways had to be swept repeatedly. The magnetic sweeper did not work well and roads had to be cleared by hand sweeping.

Damage from this and other reported incidents resulted in employees submitting more than 1000 claims. More than 800 of these were for tire damage. Repairs by the plant's garage or by a contracted local garage cost slightly over $5000.

Shortly before Christmas, Empire management decided to attempt to use interstate trucks for resupply. This largely resulted from delays in railroad deliveries caused by a derailment not related to the strike at Empire Pharmaceuticals. Trucks, escorted by Empire's security staff, at first made night entries and exits by convoys. Within a week, however, eight to twelve trucks were able to enter and leave the plant on a regularly scheduled basis without undue interference. In general, local and state police cooperated well with the Security Director in these operations.

Picket harassment at the contractor's gate caused the Empire management to seek an injunction against picketing at that entrance. No court decision was announced, however, before the strike ended. During the last several weeks of the strike contractor personnel crossed the picket line at the contractor's gate without picket confrontation. The earlier problem had resulted in part from Empire's plant engineer's attempting to use the contractor's gate for improper purposes. After the Security Director learned of the practice and forced its end, the union's militancy on this point ebbed.

Four months into the strike Empire announced that any bargaining unit employees who wanted to return to work could do so. More and more began to return. By the end of the strike, more than 400 initially striking workers had returned to work. Empire used the opportunity, however, to advertise replacement vacancies in the local newspaper. Within ten days the company hired nearly 100 new employees, advising them that the jobs were permanent. This and the return to work of a number of strikers were believed to have great affect in discouraging union members' continuing the strike.

Because the security staff was able to protect production facilities and workers and to assure shipping and receiving during the strike, production efforts remained at an acceptable fifty percent level. This was adequate for current orders. At the end of the fourth month the union realized that the company had held out, was gaining strength, and had not lost sales during the contested period.

After five months the strike ended. This resulted from much pressure on the union by its members, plus the growing back-to-work movement. In the settlement, to avoid mistakes of the earlier strike, Empire's management won a clause prohibiting the union from harassing those employees who had returned to work during the strike. This caused a much improved atmosphere in the plant following the strike. For its part, the company agreed to participate in a program to improve relations between management and union leaders to help prevent another strike in the future. The union won no further concessions in gaining strike-related goals.

Post-strike analysis by company management resulted in a number of modifications to the strike management plans. Essentially, however, most agreed that the plan had worked well and that it was the obvious preparation and determination of management to carry out that plan that deterred violence and subsequently shortened the strike.

GLOSSARY*

"A word is not a crystal, transparent and unchanged; it is the skin of a living thought and may vary greatly in color and content according to the circumstances and the time in which it is used."

—Mr. Justice Holmes
(Towne v. Eisner, 245 U.S. 418, 425-1918)

Agency Shop	—All employees in bargaining unit need not join union but must pay union dues or service charges.
Agreement, Collective	—Contract between a union and company setting forth terms of employment.
Anti-Injunction Act	—Norris-LaGuardia Act (1932). Restricted injunctions in labor disputes; banned "Yellow Dog" contracts.
Anti-Kickback Law	—Copeland Act (1934). Forbade employers' requiring workers on federally financed projects to return part of pay for right to work.
Anti-Racketeering Act	—Hobbs Act (1934). Banned extortion, force, violence in interstate commerce.
Anti-Strikebreaking Act	—Byrnes Act (1936). Barred employers' transporting strikebreakers across state lines.
Anti-Trust Act	—Sherman Act (1890). Declared illegal all conspiracies in restraint of trade or commerce. Clayton Act (1914) declared Sherman Act not applicable to labor.
Anti-Union Agreement	—See Yellow Dog Contract.

---

*Excerpts by permission from *Roberts' Dictionary of Industrial Relations, Revised Edition*, by Harold S. Roberts, copyright © 1971 by the Bureau of National Affairs, Inc., Washington, D.C. 20037.

Anti-Union Practices   —Employers' interfering with rights of self-organization and collective bargaining.

Anti-Trust Laws   —Laws limiting interference with free trade and competition; applied to labor as agencies acting in restraint of trade.

Arbitration   —Parties, unable to resolve dispute, indicate willingness to abide by decision of third party.

Arbitrator   —Individual selected by union and management to make final binding decision on basis of evidence presented in dispute.

Back-to-Work Movement   —Any organized effort to get striking employees to return to work.

Bargaining Agent   —Union certified by NLRB or a state labor agency to represent majority of employees in a bargaining unit.

Bargaining Unit   —Group of employees approved by NLRB or a state labor agency to constitute a unit for bargaining purposes.

Bergoff Technique   —Employers' hiring union members or providing outside infiltrators to disrupt unions, create dissent, foster back-to-work movements.

Blacklist   —Employers' circulating names of "undesirable" employees, often union leaders, to encourage others not to hire them. Practice now subject to unfair labor practice charge.

Blanket Injunction   —Court order so broad in its restraints that it prohibits activities beyond those of original dispute.

Boycott   —Concerted action by employers and union in refusing to do business with another employer.

Brotherhood   —Term used in older labor unions to indicate solidarity and common interests.

Byrnes Act   —See Anti-Strikebreaking Act.

Captain   —Supervisor of professional strike breakers; leader of group of pickets.

Cease and Desist Order	—Order by NLRB or state agency directing employer or union to stop an unfair labor practice.
Certification	—Recognition by NLRB or state labor agency that a union is bargaining agent for a group of employees.
Chain Picketing	—Continuous, close, moving line of pickets which prevents passage through picket line; illegal strike activity.
Check-Off	—Employer automatically deducts union dues/assessments from employees' wages and delivers to union.
Civil Rights Act of 1964	—Banned employment discrimination based on race, color, religion, sex or national origin. Applies to employers, unions, various employment agencies.
Clayton Act (1914)	—Disallowed application of anti-trust provisions of Sherman Anti-Trust Act to combinations of labor.
Closed Anti-Union Shop	—See Yellow Dog Contract; illegal under Taft-Hartley Act.
Closed Shop	—Agreement between employer and union that only union members are permitted to work; illegal under Taft-Hartley Act.
Collective Bargaining	—Process of negotiating terms and conditions of employment, administration of the agreement.
Company Spy	—Individual hired by an employer to report union activities. Outlawed by Wagner Act.
Company Union	—Labor organization of single plant or company, not affiliated with any national labor organization.
Complaint	—Formal statement by NLRB that it has *prima facia* case involving violation of labor law.
Conciliation	—Process by which parties involved in labor dispute attempt to reconcile their differences. A third party often acts as a catalyst and intermediary.

Contract   —Written agreement between employer and
                                employees' certified union setting forth
                                conditions of employment.

Cooling-Off Period   —Postponing of strike or lockout action to
                                give mediation agencies opportunity to
                                settle dispute.

Copeland Act   —See Anti-Kickback Law.

Cutback   —Unexpected reduction in work resulting
                                in layoff of employees.

Decertification   —Procedure for removing a union as the
                                certified bargaining agent for a group of
                                employees.

Discipline   —Action by employer, short of discharge,
                                against an employee for violating com-
                                pany or contract rules.

Dry-Run Picketing   —Picketing, other than during a strike, by
                                which a union brings pressure upon an
                                employer.

Duty to Bargain   —Under Taft-Hartley Act, obligation on
                                employers and union to bargain in good
                                faith to resolve labor dispute.

Economic Strike   —Work stoppage caused by disagreement
                                on wages, hours, other conditions of em-
                                ployment.

Enforced Membership   —Provision that all new company employees
                                must become union members. Same as
                                Closed Shop. Banned by Taft-Hartley Act.

Enforcement Strike   —Strike to enforce working conditions cited
                                in contract.

Enjoin   —Court action to prevent union from engag-
                                ing in strike action or requiring it or
                                employer to take some action to remedy
                                an inequity.

Espionage   —Use of spies to thwart unionization efforts
                                or to report union activity. Wagner Act
                                limited its legality.

Exclusive Bargaining Agent —The union certified by NLRB or state labor
                                agency as bargaining agent, exclusive rep-

resentative of all employees, union and non-union.

Fair Labor Standards Act (1938)	—Regulated working conditions, child labor.
Featherbedding	—Union practice of make-work arrangements favoring union members. Taft-Hartley Act made featherbedding illegal.
Federal Mediation and Conciliation Service	—Independent agency created under Taft-Hartley Act to help resolve labor disputes.
Fink	—A professional strike breaker. Finks who supervise other finks may be referred to as "nobles."
Foreman	—First line of management in the operation of a plant or facility.
General Strike	—Strike of workers throughout an entire geographical area. Not confined to any one union or industry or company.
Gentlemen's Agreement	—An agreement or understanding based solely on the good will and word of parties involved. Generally unenforcable.
Good-Faith Bargaining	—Negotiations between union and employers to reach a mutually satisfactory agreement.
Grievance	—Any complaint by an employee or union against an employer.
Grievance Adjustment	—Settling a grievance.
Grievance Committee	—Union and/or management representatives who attempt to resolve grievances.
Guaranteed Employment	—Employers' guaranteeing workers specified number of work hours per week or work days per year.
Hatch Act	—Federal Corrupt Practices Act (1947). Banned union contributions/expenditures to elect certain public officials.
Hobbs Act	—See Anti-Racketeering Act.
Hooked Man	—Worker, intentionally or unawares, engaged in espionage or surveillance activities against union. Unfair labor practice under Wagner Act (1935).

Hot Cargo —Goods produced or shipped by an employer the union has labeled "unfair."
Legality of union' sanctions against hot
cargo shipments subject to varying inter-
pretations over the years as possible illegal secondary boycotts.

Hot Goods Clause —Provisions of the Fair Labor Standards
Act prohibiting interstate shipment of
goods prepared in violation of that Act.

Illegal Strike —Any strike which has been declared unlawful under existing laws.

Industrial Disputes —Conflicts in labor-management relations
in which parties cannot resolve their
differences.

Industrial Relations —All matters affecting the relationship between workers and their employers.

Injunction —Prohibitory writ by a court restraining an
individual or group from committing an
act the court believes unfair to other parties involved.

Interstate Commerce —Trade or commerce between states; basis
for federal government's regulating labor-
management relations.

Intimidation —Effort to interfere with the rights of workers
to self-organization and collective bargain-
ing. Prohibited under federal law.

Involuntary Check-Off —Union dues deduction by employer in
which employee has no choice if he wishes
to work but in which he must give written
permission for the deduction.

Ironclad Agreement
(Contract)   —Yellow-Dog Contract. Employee agrees, as
condition of employment, that he will not
join union so long as he is an employee of
that company. Illegal under Taft-Hartley
Act.

Jim Crow Laws —Laws restricting the rights of Negroes.

Job Action —Union tactic of direct action (threats, slowdowns, walkouts, etc.) rather than use of negotiation or grievance procedures.

Journeyman	—Skilled tradesman who has successfully completed apprenticeship.
Jurisdictional Dispute	—Controversy between several unions over the right to represent certain groups or to perform certain types of work.
Jurisdictional Strike	—Work stoppage from dispute over jurisdictional claims of several unions.
Kickback	—Form of extortion by employer or union in which employee must give up part of his pay to be allowed to work.
Labor Contract	—Formal agreement resulting from collective bargaining process.
Labor Dispute	—Any controversy over terms, tenure or conditions of employment, or representation of individuals involved.
Labor Leader	—Normally applied to a person who is working full-time in the labor movement, or to one who has gained prominence in the labor field.
Labor Monopoly	—Term applied to labor unions' control over labor market to obtain benefits favorable to a particular group of employees.
Labor Movement	—General term encompassing all unions and their activities in the field of collective bargaining and social reform.
Labor Organization	—Group of workers in voluntary association to promote their mutual and individual benefits with their employers.
Labor Organizer	—Person, generally an employee of the union, assigned to a particular plant or region to recruit employees to his union.
Labor Racketeer	—Dishonest or unethical labor leader who attempts to extort funds or other favors from employers as price of maintaining peace.
Labor Relations Board	—Federal or State boards concerned primarily with handling labor relations.

Labor Spy	—Individual hired by an employer to spy on union activities and to create dissent within that union, an illegal activity.
Labor Union	—Association of wage earners for purpose of improving their working lives.
Landrum-Griffin Act	—Labor-Management Reporting & Disclosure Act of 1959. Required reporting of union finances and administrative practices.
Layoff	—Temporary or indefinite separation from employment.
Legal Sanctions	—Legal remedies or penalties applicable to employer or union where one party has violated unfair labor practices provisions of Taft-Hartley Act or appropriate state laws.
Local Union	—Basic unit of labor organization. Generally applies to a single plant unit or to a small geographical unit.
Lockout	—Employers' temporarily withholding work from employees by shutting down plant or denying entry to it to pressure for settlement of a dispute.
Majority Rule	—Provisions of federal or state laws for elections to determine who should represent employees in collective bargaining.
Make-Work Practices	—Activities of unions or individual workers to take up slack in employment or to spread available work by slowdowns or creation of unnecessary work.
Management	—Employer or company executives responsible for the administration of an enterprise and the functions of leadership within it.
Mass Picketing	—Workers' patrolling entrances or exits of a struck facility to show broad support of union's members in dispute in question.
Mediation	—Similar to "Conciliation" in that mediator attempts to bring disputants together to

	resolve an issue; difference is that in mediation that individual plays stronger, more suggestive role.
Minimum Wage	—Rate below which no employee will be paid.
Modified Closed Shop	—Contract calling for closed shop but excluding certain groups of employees from union membership. Closed shop is illegal under the Taft-Hartley Act.
National Emergency Strike	—Strike defined under Taft-Hartley Act which affects national interests and for which courts may issue an injunction.
National Industrial Recovery Act (1933)	—Established codes of compensation for employees, procedures for determining wages, work hours. Declared unconstitutional by Supreme Court in 1935.
National Labor Relations Board	—Tribunal appointed by President to certify bargaining units, establish policies regarding unfair labor practices, administer National Labor Relations Act.
National Union	—Organization bringing together many local unions within an industry or craft.
Negative Strikes	—Strikes to maintain work standards, wages, other benefits previously enjoyed by company employees but which employer has attempted to change.
Negotiation	—Meeting of employer and union to carry out collective bargaining process.
Negotiator	—Person representing union or employer in collective bargaining process.
No-Lockout Clause	—Proviso in contract in which employer agrees not to engage in lockout operation during contract period.
No-Strike Clause	—Proviso in contract in which union agrees not to strike during contract period.
Non-Union Employee	—Employee who does not belong to the particular union at his place of work.

Non-Union Shops	—Place of employment without a recognized collective bargaining agent.
Norris-LaGuardia Act	—See Anti-Injunction Act.
Open Shop	—Plant in which workers are employed regardless of union affiliation.
Open Union	—A Labor organization in which all qualified employees are permitted to join.
Organizational Picketing	—Union picketing to persuade the employer to accept that union as the bargaining agent for its employees.
Organizers	—Individuals active in recruiting employees for a union or in directing union activities.
Outlaw Strike	—A work stoppage or strike forbidden by law or called without union sanction.
Partial Strike	—Work stoppage or strike by small portion of the total organized group in a facility.
Peaceful Picketing	—Form of picketing or marching to inform employees or public that a strike is in progress or that union believes the employer engages in unfair practices.
Permanent Injunction	—Strongest of three types of injunctions court can impose in labor disputes.
Picketing	—Patrolling at or near employer's place of business during a strike or other labor dispute to give public notice of dispute or to discourage or prevent other persons from entering the facility. It is illegal to bar entrance/exit of struck facility.
Picketing at Common Site	—Picketing where employees of both a struck employer and employees of neutral employers are working. Most often found at a construction site.
Plant Rules	—Detailed working rules of an establishment.
Plant Union	—Organization of employees within a single plant.
Preferential Hiring	—Employer agrees to give preference in hiring to union members so long as the union

	can provide adequate numbers and skills needed.
Prima Facia Evidence	—Evidence sufficient on its face to establish a fact.
Primary Boycott	—Union action to prevent use of an employer's product without involving others who are not the prime individuals in the labor dispute.
Quickie Stoppage or Strike	—Spontaneous, short-lived work stoppage or strike with no advance notice to employers or, perhaps, to the union.
Racketeering	—In labor, use of unethical and extortionate force to obtain money or other favors from employers as protection against employees' actions, or from employees as protection against the employer.
Rank and File	—Individual union members who have no special status as officers or shop stewards.
Rat	—Union term applied to former union members who turn strikebreakers; sometimes applied to individuals willing to accept lower wages than those established by union scale.
Recognition	—Employer's recognition of a union as the bargaining agent among its employees.
Referee	—In a labor dispute, individual appointed by a court to gather evidence and report back to the court.
Right to Work Law	—Provisions in state laws which prohibit or make illegal arrangements between employers and unions for closed shop or other union-security provisions requiring membership in a union as a condition for employment.
Roping	—Bringing a union member, knowing or unknowing, into association with union spies for information on union activities.
Rough Shadowing	—Keeping a man under surveillance in such

	manner that he knows he is being watched and is intimidated.
Sabotage	—Direct action by employees to injure or destroy an employer's income or property.
Salaried Employee	—A worker who does not receive an hourly or an incentive rate of pay.
Scab	—Union term for an employee who continues to work while a strike is in progress or who accepts employment during a strike.
Secondary Boycott	—Pressure by a union on a neutral party who then exerts pressure against the person who is the actual adversary, such as refusal to handle products of a company which is dealing with a struck employer.
Secondary Picketing	—Bringing pressure by picketing an establishment not directly involved in a labor dispute but which has some business connection with the company with whom the union does have a dispute.
Secondary Strike	—Strike against an employer who deals with a company whose workers are on strike.
Self-Organization	—Protected rights of employees to band for obtaining better wages, hours, working conditions.
Settlement	—Agreement resolving a particular labor dispute.
Sherman Act	—See Anti-Trust Act of 1890.
Shop	—A place where work is done.
Shop Chairman	—The union's chief steward in a plant.
Shop Committee	—Small group of union workers who represent all employees in handling grievances.
Shop Steward	—Union Steward. Representative of the union who carries out responsibilities of the union in that plant at the department level.
Sit-Down Strike	—Work stoppage in which employees refuse to work or to leave premises.
Skilled Labor	—Workers who have mastered one of the traditional crafts.

Slowdown	—Deliberate effort by employees to reduce production and efficiency to obtain concessions from an employer.
Soldiering	—Loafing or deliberate time wasting; loss of production by an employee. Generally does not involve other employees and is not to exert pressure on an employer.
Speed-Up	—Efforts by employers to increase productivity without corresponding compensation.
Stay-In Strike	—Strike during which employees remain in plant; a prolonged sit-down strike may become a stay-in strike.
Stool Pigeon	—Labor term for company spy.
Straw Boss	—Worker who takes the lead in small group's activities.
Strike	—Temporary stoppage of work or withdrawal from work to express a grievance or to enforce labor demands.
Strike Benefits	—Union payments to strikers to help finance them during work stoppages.
Strike Fund	—Union fund reserve put aside to defray strike expenses.
Strikebreaker	—A person, not a regular employee, who accepts work in a struck facility.
Supervisor	—A person who has management responsibilities, usually including the right to hire or fire.
Sweatshop	—A place of work where the conditions are substantially sub-standard.
Taft-Hartley Act	—Labor-Management Relations Act of 1947. Cited numerous restrictions on union practices.
Temporary Restraining Order	—See Injunction.
Trade Union	—Association of workers in a particular trade or craft to promote common interests in work benefits.
Turnout	—Strike.
Umpire	—See "Arbitrator."

Unauthorized Strike — A strike which does not have the approval of the union and is in violation of a no-strike provision of the current contract. Referred to as a wildcat, illegal, quickie or outlaw strike.

Unfair Employer — Employer guilty of unfair labor practices under federal or state labor laws or one who refuses to recognize a union or to employ its members.

Unfair Labor Practices — Activities specifically prohibited under federal or state labor laws.

Union Leadership — Union members responsible for guiding programs of their organization.

Union Membership — All individuals who are members of a union.

Union Security Clauses — Contract agreements securing the union against employers, non-union employees, and/or raids by competing unions. Typical would be the Union Shop.

Union Shop — A form of union security agreement by which an employer can hire whomever he wishes but requires him to join the union within thirty days and to remain a member or pay dues or other assessments.

Union Steward — See "Shop Steward."

Unskilled Labor — Called "common labor." Person performing simple manual operations, easily learned and requiring limited skill.

Vested Rights — Rights of a financial nature, such as participating in an employer's pension plan.

Wagner-Connery Act — National Labor Relations Act of 1935. Established right of employees to organize, bargaining unit's certification, defined unfair labor practices.

Walkout — Strike. Usually, however, more akin to a quickie or wildcat strike as no formal notification to employer or to union.

Wildcat Strike — See "Unauthorized or Outlaw Strike."

Yellow-Dog Contract — An agreement (oral or written) between an employer and a worker that, as a condition of employment, worker will not join a union or, if he already is a union member, that he will leave the union. Under the Norris-LaGuardia Act, Yellow-Dog Contracts are not enforcable.

BIBLIOGRAPHY

1. For a more detailed discussion see pamphlet, *Employer's Labor Relations Guidebook*, Human Resources Division, Indiana State Chamber of Commerce, 1 North Capitol, Indianapolis, Indiana 46204, p. 3, 1980.
2. *Ibid.*, p. 26.
3. For a more detailed discussion see pamphlet, *Management and Strikes*, Human Resources Division, Indiana State Chamber of Commerce, *Ibid.*, p. 6, Undated.
4. *Ibid.*, p. 12.
5. *Ibid.*, p. 17.
6. *Ibid.*, pp. 26–29.
7. *Ibid.*, p. 11.

INDEX